he Development of International Arbitration on Bilateral Investment Treaties

s Between States and Investor, ICSID Cases Against Turkey Regarding Energy Sector

Zeynep Akgul

DISSERTATION.COM

Boca Raton

The Development of International Arbitration on Bilateral Investment Trea...
Disputes Between States and Investor, ICSID Cases Against Turkey Regarding Ene...
ector

Dissertation.com
Boca Raton, Florida
USA • 2008

ISBN-10: 1-59942-669-2
ISBN-13: 978-1-59942-669-3

THE DEVELOPMENT OF INTERNATIONAL ARBITRATION ON
BILATERAL INVESTMENT TREATIES: DISPUTES BETWEEN STATES
AND INVESTOR, ICSID CASES AGAINST TURKEY REGARDING ENERGY
SECTOR

Submitted by

AKGUL ZEYNEP

LLM for International Business Law, 2007

THE DEVELOPMENT OF INTERNATIONAL ARBITRATION ON BILATERAL INVESTMENT TREATIES: DISPUTES BETWEEN STATES AND INVESTOR, ICSID CASES AGAINST TURKEY REGARDING ENERGY SECTOR

Submitted by **Zeynep AKGUL** to the University of Exeter as a dissertation towards the degree of Master of Law by advanced study in International Business Law, September 2007.

Dissertation Supervisor: Professor Andrew Tettenborn

This dissertation is dedicated to the memory of my uncle Av. Akad Ozbek who inspired me to pursue academic career, and my family, and my dear husband for his encouragement and support...

ABSTRACT

This dissertation analyses developments of international arbitration on investment disputes. Recent years, there has been an extraordinary increase in the number of investment arbitration for breach of Bilateral Investment Treaties (BITs). These treaties include substantive and procedural rules to provide investment security and investment neutrality to foreign investor. In particular, most BITs have investor-state dispute settlement provision which allows investors to sue host states directly. Through analyzing the Turkish BIT experience, this study concludes that there are different approaches that utilized in various investor-state dispute settlement provisions. Thus, the wording of these provisions is important. Furthermore, the ICSID arbitration is mostly incorporated into BITs dispute settlement provisions since the ICSID arbitration has an effective system and different characteristics from other types of international commercial arbitration. This dissertation examines not only the main features of the ICSID, but also the recent amendments made to the ICSID arbitration rules. Finally, after analyzing the concluded and pending ICSID cases against Turkey regarding energy sector, this study concludes that the ICSID has an important role for the development of the international arbitration on investment disputes.

CONTENT

INTRODUCTION

It is true that in recent years foreign investment is increasing among countries all around the world. The most important thing is that the parties who are involving foreign investment transactions have different interests and rights. For example, the main interest of investors is the profit in these transactions. On the other hand, the aim of host states is to develop their economy. As we can rightly argue that every party has different interests so probably there will be disputes in their negotiations and contracts. Thus, effective international dispute settlement mechanism is needed for investment disputes. For this reason, we seek to focus on investor-state dispute settlement procedure in our dissertation.

The proliferation of Bilateral Investment Treaties (BITs) which include investor-state dispute settlement provisions has an important role in the development of international investment arbitration. Thus, in the first chapter, we analyze what constitutes BITs and what are their impacts on international investment arbitration.

In the second chapter, we examine what are the investor-state dispute settlement provisions in the BITs in order to show our reader how these provisions are effected the international investment arbitration. In particular, this study analyzes these provisions of BITs that Turkey signed with other Countries. In fact, Turkey signed several BITs which have different approaches with many countries. Moreover, the recent developments on investor-state dispute settlement procedures under BITs will be explained in the same chapter.

In the third chapter, we explain the main characteristics of ICSID arbitration to clarify how important is choosing ICSID rules while solving the dispute under the BITs. Also we will mention some discrepancies of ICSID provision from other arbitral procedures in order to show the efficiency of the ICSID procedure. In addition, we will analyze the amendments made to the arbitration rules of the ICSID on April 10, 2006.

Finally, in our last chapter we will explain and analyze concluded and pending ICSID cases against Turkey regarding energy sector so as to illustrate the importance and the practical aspects of the main requirements of investor-state dispute settlement procedures.

CHAPTER 1   Bilateral Investment Treaties and International Arbitration

I.   Overview of BITs

Foreign investment plays an important role in economic development. Mostly developing countries want to encourage foreign investment in their countries. When foreign investor invests in host country, he may encounter so many risks. The followings are some of the risks that foreign investor will face to face: His investment may be unlawfully expropriate or nationalize by host country, or there might be currency transfer restrictions in the host states. The other thing is that the treatment of investment will be changed after the establishment of investment. The host country may treat national investor more favourable than foreign investor. These situations may affect foreign investor badly since there will be no competition at that time. In order to protect its investment from these kinds of risks, foreign investors should rely on some laws in particular international investment law. However, international investment law still continues to develop for foreign investment. Since there is no multinational treaty on investment, bilateral investment treaties are the main sources of international investment law.[1]

Bilateral investment treaties (BITs) are usually signed between two countries. These countries can be one developed country and the other one developing country but recently this tradition has changed and BITs can be signed between two developing and two developed countries.[2] This chapter plans to explain firstly, what the overview of the BITs is secondly, the impact of BITs on international investment law and finally, the development of international arbitration in international investment disputes.

A.   The Aim of BITs

As the main sources of international investment law, BITs provide investment security and investment neutrality to foreign investment.[3] In other words they include provisions which address above mentioned foreign investments risks. Most BITs have similar provisions and the following issues can be found most of the BITs: Preamble investment and investor definitions, treatment of investment, expropriation, currency

---

[1] United Nations Conference on Trade and Development (UNCTAD), Bilateral Investment Treaties 1995-2006: Trends In Investment Rule Making, United Nations, New York and Geneva, 2007, p. 1.
[2] Loibl Gerhard, International Economic Law, Evans D. Malcolm (Ed.), International Law, Second Edition, 2006,p.710.
[3] Vandevelde J. Kenneth, Investment Liberalization and Economic Development: The Role of Bilateral Investment Treaties, Colombia Journal of Transnational Law, 1998, p.507-514.

transfer, subrogation and dispute settlement provisions.[4] The main goal of developing countries signing BITs or negotiating BITs is to attract foreign investment as a means of fostering economic growth and development. On the other hand, the purpose of BITs for the developed countries is to obtain legal protection for investment and preclude non-commercial risks facing foreign investors in host countries.[5] Indeed, BITs' original name is agreement signed between two countries concerning the reciprocal promotion and protection of investment. It must be noted that most BITs do not explain which contracting party is the source of the investment or which is the recipient. [6] Thus, the promotion and the protection of investment are reciprocal.

B.   The Origin of BITs

Before briefly analysing the substance of the BITs, it is necessary to explain the origin of the BITs. BITs can be deemed as a successor to the friendship commerce and navigation treaties (FCNs).[7] In particular, the USA negotiated and signed FCNs with many European states including France, Italy and Latin American states so as to improve and to protect foreign trade relationships with each other.[8] These treaties provided international legal standard for the protection of natural and legal persons.[9] However, they did not directly include investment issues. Thus, European countries realized that there should be treaties that address investment related issues. After this, most European countries commenced to sign BITs with developing countries. It should be noted that the first modern BIT signed between Germany and Pakistan in 1959.[10] Recently, the number of BITs and the number of countries signing these treaties have increased. The numbers of BITs have reached almost 2,500 at the end of 2005.[11]

BITs have substantive and procedural rules that secure foreign investment. Although every BIT covers the same issues, there are many exceptions and reservations.

---

[4] Sornaraj M., The International Law on Foreign Investment, Second Edition, Cambridge University Press, 2004, p.217.
[5] Dolzer Rudolf & Stevens Margrete, Bilateral Investment Treaties, Martinus Nijhoff Publishers, 1995, p.12.
[6] Siquerios Jose Luis, Bilateral Treaties on the Reciprocal Protection of Foreign Investment, California Western International Law Journal, Spring 1994, p.257.
[7] Sornaraj op.cit., p. 209.
[8] Vandevelde J Kenneth, The BIT Program: A Fifteen-Year Appraisal, The Development and Expansion of Bilateral Investment Treaties, American Society of International Law Proceedings, 1992, p. 533.
[9] Sornaraj op.cit., p. 209.
[10] Treaty for the Promotion and Protection of Investments, Pakistan-F.R.G., 457 U.N.T.S. 23, Lauterpacht Elihu, International Law and Private Foreign Investment, Indiana Journal of Global Legal Studies, Spring 1997, p.266.
[11] UNCTAD op.cit., p. 1.

In this dissertation, we will analyse investor-state dispute settlement procedure. However, most of the investment disputes are related with expropriation, most favourite nation principle, and national treatment issues which are essential substantive rules of the BITs. Thus, it is important to explain them briefly.

a. Expropriation

Most BITs include a clause on expropriation and compensation in order to protect investors against the risk of unlawful expropriation. In expropriation clauses, each contracting party agrees not to take any measures directly or indirectly for expropriation or nationalization or any other comparable measures effecting foreign investment made in its territory by nationals of the other contracting party. The BIT between Turkey and China is an example of an expropriation clause utilized in numerous BITs: "*1. The investments made by nationals or companies of one contracting party in the territory of the other contracting party shall not be expropriated or nationalized or subjected to other measures having a similar effect, unless the following conditions are fulfilled:*

   (a)   *The measures are adopted for public purpose, within the framework of its laws and regulations.*

   (b)   *The measures are not discriminatory.*"[12]

It is true that most expropriation clauses require the measure should be non-discriminatory, for a public purpose, against payment of prompt, adequate and effective compensation and with regard for the due process of law.[13] Due to the fact that there are various disputes regarding indirect expropriations or regulatory takings, some countries such as the USA and Canada redraft their model BITs to include specific provisions on indirect expropriations.[14]

b. National Treatment

Most BITs include provisions requiring each party to accord the foreign investor the same treatment that host state accords to its nationals.[15] Pursuant to these provisions, each contracting party ensures that the investments receive national treatment. For example, the BIT between Nigeria and Turkey provides that "Each Party

---

[12] See Article 3 of the Agreement between The People's Republic of China and The Republic of Turkey Concerning The Reciprocal Promotion and Protection of Investments, http://www.unctad.org/sections/dite/iia/docs/bits/china_turkey.pdf (visited 20.6.2007).
[13] Dolzer & Stevens op.cit., p. 97.
[14] UNCTAD op.cit., p 52.
[15] Dolzer & Stevens op.cit., p. 63.

shall accord to these investments, once established, treatment no less favourable than that accorded in similar situation to investments of its investors or to investment of investors of any third country, whichever is the most favourable."[16] The aim of National Treatment provision is to promote investment neutrality. National treatment means that the contracting parties should give investors of the other contracting party a treatment no less favourable than the treatment they grant to investments of their own investors. Thus, the host state will not discriminate among investors based on nationality. However, it should be noted that there are exceptions to the national treatment.[17]

c. Most Favourite Nation Treatment

Most BITs contain most favourite nation treatment (MFN) provision which means that suppose Italy and Spain signed a BIT, Turkey which is not a contracting party of this BIT but signed another BIT with Spain which provides MFN clause, at this situation, if Turkish investor made an investment in Spain and he can rely on one of the Italy-Spain BIT clause which gives extra protection to the Italian investors. If there is MFN clause in the BIT, both of the countries' investors can depend on other BIT clauses which give more protection or right to other countries' investors.

The question will arise whether the scope of MFN clauses in a BIT apply to dispute resolution provisions or not.[18] In other words, it can be possible for the investors to utilize MFN clause to establish jurisdiction over their investment disputes with host states. This problem will commonly occur, for instance, if the claimant investor fails to fulfil requirement in the investor-State dispute settlement provisions of the applicable BIT. It should be noted that the scope of the MFN clauses is controversial issue in recent ICSID arbitration cases.

The problem was addressed in *Maffezini*[19], *Salini*[20] and *Plama*[21] cases. In *Maffezini* case, the tribunal held that Mr. Maffezini was allowed to use the dispute settlement provisions of the BIT between Chile and Spain because the MFN clause of

---

[16] Article II of the Agreement between The Republic of Turkey and The Federal Republic of Nigeria Concerning The Reciprocal Promotion and Protection of Investments, http://www.unctad.org/sections/dite/iia/docs/bits/turkey_nigeria.pdf (visited 20.6.2007).

[17] See exceptions for Most Favoured Nation Treatment.

[18] Fietta Stephen, Most Favoured Nation Treatment and Dispute Resolution Under Bilateral Investment Treaties: A Turning Point, International Arbitration Law Review, 2005, 131-138.

[19] ICSID Case No. ARB/97/7, Decision of January 25, 2000.

[20] ICSID Case No. ARB/02/13, Decision of November 15, 2004.

[21] ICSID Case No. ARB/03/24, Decision of February 8, 2005.

the BIT between Argentina and Spain is broad and precisely refers to "all matters subject to this agreement".[22] On the other hand, in *Salini* and *Plama* cases, the ICSID Tribunal found that the MFN clauses of the applicable BITs were not intended to extend to dispute settlement provisions. This new approach taken by ICSID Tribunals summarized in the *Plama* case. Paragraph 223 of the *Plama* case points out that: "*. . . the principle with multiple exceptions as stated by the tribunal in the Maffezini case should instead be a different principle with one, single exception; an MFN provision in a basic treaty does not incorporate by reference dispute settlement provisions in whole or in part set forth in another treaty, unless the MFN provision in the basic treaty leaves no doubt that the Contracting Parties intended to incorporate them*".

After analyzing these three ICSID cases' outcome, it can be discovered that the claimant investor can only utilize MFN clauses to apply for the more favourable dispute resolution provisions of BITs with third states, if the Contracting Parties had an intention for this possibility. Thus, the wording of MFN clauses is really important. For example the UK Model BIT illustrates the intention of the parties to incorporate investor-State dispute Settlement provisions into a BIT through MFN clauses. Indeed, Article 3 (3) of the UK Model BIT states that: "*For avoidance of doubt it is confirmed that the treatment (MFN) provided for in paragraphs (1) and (2) above shall apply to the provisions of Articles 1 to 11 of this Agreement (It should be noted that Articles 8 and 9 of the UK Model BIT set out dispute settlement provisions)*"[23]

The aim of MFN provision is also to promote investment neutrality. Since it is a non-discrimination provision, the host country is obliged to not discriminate among investments and investors based on nationality.[24] Moreover, most BITs include some exceptions to MFN obligations. For instance, regional economic integration agreement such as custom union is the most essential exception that undermines the non-discrimination provisions.[25]

---

[22] UNCTAD, p.39.
[23] Fietta Stephen op.cit., p.136.
[24] Vandevelde, op.cit., p.512.
[25] See Article 2 of the Turkey-Tunisia BITs, Agreement between The Republic of Tunisia and The Republic of Turkey Concerning The Reciprocal Promotion and Protection of Investments, http://www.unctad.org/sections/dite/iia/docs/bits/TurkeyTunisia.pdf (20.6.2007).

d. Dispute Settlement Provisions

As we mentioned above there is not only substantive rules but also procedural rules to protect investors. Most BITs include dispute settlement provisions for both state-state disputes and investor-state disputes. Each treaty includes that unless the dispute cannot be resolved through the diplomatic way, parties can submit the dispute to the arbitration with regard to the dispute settlement provision in the BIT.[26] These two different types of settlement provisions are always written in two separate clauses. Nevertheless, it is essential to note that there is no uniformity between most of the BITs in particular at the dispute resolution parts. Thus, since the dispute settlement provisions are different, it will be more convenient to discuss them separately. First we will slightly explain what constitutes state-state dispute settlement provision in the BITs and in the next chapter we will deeply analyse the investor-state dispute resolution provisions in the BITs which are extremely important issues to understand the development of international arbitration on BITs for our dissertation.

1. State-State Dispute Settlement Provision

Before instituting formal proceedings, parties are required to solve the dispute by consolidation. If they cannot be successful to settle the dispute, with regard to their request the dispute is submitted to the ad hoc arbitration tribunal. The tribunal will be created from two arbitrators; each one will be selected from one of the parties independently and the third arbitrator from a third country will be appointed by either both of the parties or by the selected arbitrators.[27] If parties cannot reach an agreement regarding the selection of the arbitrators, the President of the International Court of Justice will make the appointments.[28] Numerous BITs which are signed between Turkey and the other countries proved that state-state dispute settlement provisions in these BITs are written almost same language and same procedure.[29] Therefore, it can be said that there is uniformity with regard to this provision.

---

[26] Vandevelde op.cit., p.508.
[27] Article 7 of the Turkey-USA BITs provides settlement disputes between contracting parties. Turkey-United States: Treaty Concerning the Reciprocal Encouragement and Protection of Investments, http://www.unctad.org/sections/dite/iia/docs/bits/us_turkey.pdf (visited 20.6.2007).
[28] *Ibid.* Article 7.
[29] See Article 7 of Turkey-United Kingdom, Agreement for the Promotion and Protection of Investments, and also see Article 9 of Turkey-Tunisia BIT.

II.   The Impact of BITs on International Investment Law

BITs improved international investment law in two ways one is the subject matter of international law, and the protection of shareholders.[30] In fact international law does not recognize private companies as international subjects but with BITs, this is changed. Through BITs, private companies and natural persons can directly sue states. Thus, BITs have become extremely important because of the investor-state dispute settlement provisions. For this reason, investor-state dispute settlement provisions are our main topic to clarify the development of international arbitration on BITs. Moreover, BITs established a new and special regime for the protection of shareholders who are not under the protection of international law.[31]

BITs allow States to enact investment laws but at the same time it provides that any rights in the agreement should not be interfered by any investment rules.[32] In fact, BITs can affect domestic legislation. Countries enacted or amended their domestic laws in order to establish the harmony with BITs. As an example, Professor Mutharika states in his study that in 1993 Zambia government abolished the 1991 code and enacted a new code that permits payments in order to be similar with those that was given in the Zambia-Germany BIT.[33]

BITs have an important role as a source in negotiations of recent regional and multilateral treaties.[34] For instance, BITs influenced the embodiment of the World Bank Group Guidelines on the Treatment of Foreign Direct Investment, subjected in September 1992 by the Joint Ministerial Development Committee of the World Bank and the IMF.[35] In addition, the North American Free Trade Agreement Investment (NAFTA) Chapter (Chapter 11) provides similar provisions in line with the most of the BITs.

---

[30] Caliskan Yusuf, The Development of International Investment Law: Lessons From The OECD MAI Negotiations And Their Application to a Possible Multilateral Agreement on Investment, Washington University School of Law, Jurist Science Doctorate (JSD) Dissertation, 2002, p.55.

[31] Kishoiyian Bernard, The Utility of Bilateral Investment Treaties in the Formulation of Customary International law, Nortwestern Journal of International Law and Business, Winter 1994, p.350; Sornaraj op.cit., p.228.

[32] Caliskan Yusuf op.cit., p.56.

[33] Mutharika A. Peter, Creating an Attractive Investment Climate in the Common Market for Eastern and Southern Africa (COMESA) Region, Foreign Investment Law Journal, ICSID Review, 1997, p.272.

[34] Caliskan Yusuf op.cit., p.56.

[35] Dolzer & Stevens, op.cit., p. xii-xiii.

III. The Development of International Arbitration in International Investment Disputes

Recently international arbitration has become an important dispute settlement mechanism for foreign investors' interests to resolve disputes with government entities and to recover losses caused by states' action.[36] Before explaining this recent phenomenon, it is good to analyse previously often used adjudication mechanisms. The protection of the property rights of aliens has been one of the main issues of the international law. In particular, a state is entitled to exercise diplomatic protection for its nationals who are injured by acts of another state.[37] In order to benefit from diplomatic protection, foreigners should be unable to obtain satisfaction through local remedies.

Indeed, under customary international law a foreign investor is required to recourse the disputes in the host state courts.[38] If a foreign investor will not get effective remedies from court, an investor seek to diplomatic protection from its home country. Nonetheless, there are deficiencies of diplomatic protection remedies.[39] First, as a mater of its policy home country may choose not to exercise diplomatic protection, since it does not want to lose international relationship with the host country.[40] Second, even the home country successfully recourses an investors claim, it is not legally oblige to give the proceeds of the claim to its national.[41] Third, it is difficult to determine the multinational corporations' nationality. Thus, the question will rise which state has the right of diplomatic protection.

Knowing these discrepancies, foreign investors often refused diplomatic protection and they prefer to submit their disputes to the commercial arbitration. In fact, international commercial arbitration also provides a forum for the resolution of disputes involving a state. However, foreign investor can recourse their disputes to international commercial arbitration process, only if state granted its consent to arbitration by contract.[42] In practise the concessions contract between investor and state incorporate consent to arbitration in dispute settlement clauses, but this consent is only granted

---

[36] Caruba L. Sandra, Resolving International Investment Disputes in a Globalised World, New Zealand Business Law Quarterly, June 2007, p.128-130.; Gottwald Eric, Leveling The Playing Field: Is It Time for a Legal Assistance Center for Developing Nations in Investment Treaty Arbitration?, American University International Law Review, 2007, p.246-247.
[37] Don R.Y, Protection of Foreign Investment under International Law, 1979, p.396.
[38] UNCTAD, Dispute Settlement: Investor-State, 2003, p.5.
[39] Ibid, p. 6
[40] Ibid.
[41] Ibid.
[42] Collins Lawrence, Morse C G J, McClean David, Briggs Adrian, Harris Jonathan, McLachlan Campbell, Dicey, Morris & Collins on the Conflict of Laws, 14th Edition, Sweet & Maxwell, 2006, p 779.

within the scope of the concession agreement and it will not cover other investment issues. Thus, a foreign investor can only pursue litigation in host country. This situation creates problems for foreign investor since the host state can object to jurisdiction of the court or claim state immunity.[43] Due to the fact that above mentioned problems in international commercial arbitration and pursuing the diplomatic protection, the foreign investor needs to have a specific investor state dispute settlement mechanism.

Indeed there are two important developments in international investment law for efficient investor-state dispute settlement mechanisms. Firstly, the establishment of International Centre for the Settlement of Investment Disputes (ICSID) as an arbitral institution is the starting point for the development of arbitration in international investment disputes. The executive directors of the World Bank adopted the text of the Convention on the Settlement of Investment Disputes between States and Nationals of Other states.[44] On 18 March 1965 after its ratification by 20 states the ICSID Convention entered into force on 14 October in 1966.

The main aim of this convention is to facilitate foreign investment through the creation of a favourable investment climate. In recent years the number of investor state arbitrations under the ICSID has increased.[45] Furthermore, this proliferation in investment arbitration under ICSID rules caused the institution to amend ICSID rules on 10 April 2006. Thus, this study will explain at Chapter 3 not only the main issues of the ICSID proceedings but also the recent amendments of ICSID rules.

Secondly, the immense growth in the conclusion of BITs and regional investment treaties, most of which provide for the compulsory arbitration of investor-state disputes have main role in the development of arbitration in international investment disputes.[46] As explained above most BITs have common substantive and procedural provisions. These treaties generally provide national treatment, most favourite nation treatment, fair and equitable treatment, protection against expropriation without compensation and dispute settlement mechanisms. It is true that most BITs contain investor-state arbitration provisions which allow foreign investors to sue states directly for the violation of investors' treaty rights. Moreover, the NAFTA and the Energy Charter Treaty also provide investor state dispute settlement procedure.

---

[43] *Ibid.*
[44] The text of the Convention is published in 575 United Nations Treaty Series159, 4 International Legal Materials 524 (1965). See http://www.worldbank.org/icsid/basicdoc/basicdoc.htm
[45] Harten Van Gus, Loughlin Martin, Investment Treaty Arbitration As a Species of Global Administrative Law, European Journal of International Law, February 2006, p.124
[46] Harten Van Gus, Loughlin Martin, op. cit., p.123; Caruba op.cit., p.136; Gottwald op.cit., p.248.

In this dissertation, we will analyse the BITs' investor-state dispute settlement provisions. It is true that the number of investment treaty arbitration disputes registered at the ICSID and other international arbitration mechanisms has increased in recent years. For example, the number of known claims was 219 in year 2005 while it was 75 in 2000.[47]

---

[47] Gottwald op.cit., p.247.

CHAPTER 2   **Dispute Settlements between Investor and State**

I.   General Information on Dispute Settlements between Investor and State

The most important part of the BITs is investor versus state dispute settlement mechanism which is a common characteristic of all BITs. The dispute resolution provisions provide the protection of investors who do not have to depend on diplomatic protection of their countries. Being sure from the compliance of the host countries' obligations stipulated in the BITs makes investors feel confident about investment in that country. Another advantage of this mechanism is the separation of the legal and political issues, since it ensures that disputes are solved in the legal ground.[48] It is also true that a great deal of BITs prevent contracting party from applying the diplomatic protection, while the investor-state arbitral proceeding is still processing.

Most BITs provides general provisions about investor-state dispute settlement mechanism. In fact, most BITs include the following limited issues: stating different arbitration venues which are suitable for the investors, the appointment of arbitrator's procedure, and the obligation of contracting parties regarding the enforcement of arbitration award. Therefore, we can say that various procedural issues with respect to arbitration are not mentioned in most of the BITs. The clarification of other procedural issues can be done only by referring the arbitration rules which existing in ICSID or UNCITRAL.[49]

Recently, an increasing amount of BITs has mentioned investor state dispute settlement provisions more deeply. To clarify, BITs have provided guidance to the disputing parties concerning arbitration procedures and increased the strength of these adjudication mechanisms. In particular, it is obvious that Chapter 11 of the NAFTA has affected these BITs significantly. It is worth while to note that in particular Model BITs of Canada and USA have followed the same approach of the NAFTA Chapter 11.

However, not all of the BITs have same comprehensive investor versus state dispute settlement provisions. The minority of the BITs includes specific information about investor-state dispute settlement provisions but the most of them still continues with the traditional approach and still depends on international arbitration regulations to clarify specific procedural aspects. To analyze these approaches deeply, it will be useful to divide the subject into two parts; first we will focus on rules that are main

---

[48] UNCTAD op.cit, p. 100.
[49] *Ibid.* p. 100.

requirements of the investor-state dispute settlement procedures and later we will examine the development of new trends at the investor-state disputes settlement procedures.

II.   Main Requirements in Investor State Dispute Settlement Provisions

Developed countries include main requirements for investor-State dispute settlement mechanism in numerous BITs so as to provide its investors more secure environment. The main requirements that mostly stipulated in BITs can be analyzed through following headings: Definition of investment disputes, legal standing, preconditions for the dispute settlement mechanism, the forum of arbitration, applicable law and enforcement of arbitral awards.

A.   Definition of Investment Disputes

The definition of "investment disputes" is one of the controversial issues that might be raised in arbitration proceedings. To apply international investment arbitration, the subject of dispute must be investment. The definition of investment disputes differs from one BIT to another one. These discrepancies might have an essential effect on the kind of disputes which are submitted to arbitration. Thus, it is important to define what kind of investment that investors are able to submit to international arbitration under the BITs. [50] For instance, in Turkey-the Netherlands BIT the definition of investment dispute stipulated as a dispute involving "(a) the interpretation or application of any investment authorization granted by a contacting party's foreign investment authority to an investor of the other contracting party; or (b) a breach of any right conferred or created by this agreement with respect to an investment."[51]

Furthermore, in the Article VI of the US-Turkey BIT, the definition of "investment dispute" also covers a dispute involving "the interpretation of application of an investment agreement between a Party and a national or company of the other party". After analyzing these two treaty provisions, it can be discovered that if the definition of investment dispute is broad such as in the above mentioned Article VI of

---

[50] Freyer Dana H., Garfinkel Barry H., Bilateral Investment Treaties and Arbitration, Dispute Resolution Journal, 1998, p. 75.
[51] Article 8 (1) (a) (b) of the Agreement on Reciprocal Encouragement and Protection of Investments between the Kingdom of the Netherlands and the Republic of Turkey BIT, http://www.unctad.org/sections/dite/iia/docs/bits/netherlands_turkey.pdf (Visited 20.6.2007).

the US-Turkey BIT, this will lead to the ability of utilizing the arbitration for any breach of an investment agreement. Moreover, in most of the recent US BITs, investment dispute defined as broad as it could be. For example; in the US-Argentina BIT, the investment dispute is defined as "a dispute between a party and a national company of the other party arising out of or relating to an investment agreement."[52]

As mentioned above broad definition of investment dispute is extremely important for investors since if disputes are specifically defined, a huge amount of possibilities may be left out of the agreement. For this reason, most of the investors may not seek to invest in the country which has signed such an agreement. Therefore, the broad definition of investment dispute creates the trend which is preferable between most of countries.

Some other BITs embrace investor-state dispute resolution provisions which are applicable to disputes that are directly related to a "covered investment".[53] This is the most common approach in most of the BITs, despite there are discrepancies when it is looked through deeply in the details. In particular, there are differences in the clauses that define which types of disputes are suitable to application of investor-state dispute settlement procedure. The followings are the examples of different wordings in the dispute settlement clauses: disputes arising "in connection with" an investment, "arising out" of an investment, "with respect" to an investment, "concerning" an investment or "related to" an investment.[54] For example, Turkey-Russia BIT states that "1. Any dispute between a Contracting Party and an investor of the other Contracting Party *arising in connection with investment activities*,"[55] Moreover, Bilateral Investment Treaty between Turkey and Algeria states that "1. Disputes between one of the Parties and one investor of the other Party, *in connection with his investment*, shall be notified in writing, including detailed information, by the investor to the recipient Party of the investment."[56] In addition, Turkey-United Kingdom BITs defines disputes "an alleged breach of any conferred or created by this Agreement *with respect to an investment*."[57]

[52] See Article Article VII (1) of the Treaty Between the United States of America and the Argentine Republic Concerning the Reciprocal Encouragement and Protection of Investment, http://www.unctad.org/sections/dite/iia/docs/bits/argentina_us.pdf (visited 22.8.2007).
[53] UNCTAD, op.cit., p.102.
[54] *Ibid.* p.102.
[55] See Article X (1) of the Agreement between the Government of the Russian Federation and the Government of the Republic of Turkey regarding the Promotion and Reciprocal Protection of Investments, http://www.unctad.org/sections/dite/iia/docs/bits/russia_turkey.pdf (Visited 20.6.2007).
[56] See Article VII of the Agreement between The Government of The Republic of Turkey and The Government of The Democratic and Popular Republic of Algeria Concerning The Reciprocal Promotion

It is essential to note that as it is in the drafting an arbitration clause, the wording of the clause is an extremely important issue for investor-state dispute settlement provisions on BITs. Indeed, the scope of an arbitration agreement should be stated precisely in an arbitration clause because an arbitration agreement gives a mandate to an arbitral tribunal to decide about all disputes which can occur within the ambit of that agreement. In fact an arbitrator could not give a decision which goes beyond this mandate. If he does, his award will be rejected recognition and enforcement under the provisions of the New York Convention.[58] Therefore, like an arbitration agreement, BITs should include clear provisions on investor-state disputes. Although national courts, ICSID and other international arbitration institutions do not construe the scope of dispute narrowly which was stipulated in the BITs, parties still have the responsibility of drafting wide range of disputes.

Some BITs restricts the application of the investor-state dispute settlement procedures to "one or very few" obligations in the BITs.[59] For example, if the BITs provision regarding investor-state only permit the investor to submit the dispute with respect to the amount of compensation resulting from expropriation, the investor can recourse only expropriation dispute to investor-state dispute settlement procedure. Thus, this situation limits the application and effectiveness of investor-state dispute settlement mechanism. For example, agreement between China and Turkey provides in Article VII (b) that "*If a dispute involving the amount of the compensation resulting from an expropriation or nationalization referred to in Article III cannot be settled within one year from the date upon which the dispute arose, it may be submitted to an ad hoc arbitral tribunal for settlement in accordance with the Arbitration rules of UNCITRAL by each party subject to the dispute.*"[60]

This is mean that the investor is permitted to apply the investor-state dispute settlement provisions, only if the dispute arises from the amount of compensation which

and Protection of Investments, http://www.unctad.org/sections/dite/iia/docs/bits/turkey_algeria.pdf (visited 20.6.2007).

[57] See Article 8 (1) (c) of the Agreement between The Government of The United Kingdom of Great Britain and Northern Ireland and The Government of The Republic of Turkey for The Promotion and Protection of Investments, http://www.unctad.org/sections/dite/iia/docs/bits/uk_turkey.pdf (visited 20.6.2007).

[58] Redfern Alan, Hunter Martin, Law and Practice of International Commercial Arbitration, Fourth Edition, London, 2004, Sweet and Maxwell, p.153.

[59] UNCTAD op.cit., p.103.

[60] See Article VII (b) of the Agreement between The People's Republic of China The Republic of Turkey Concerning The Reciprocal Promotion and Protection of Investments, http://www.unctad.org/sections/dite/iia/docs/bits/china_turkey.pdf (visited 20.6.2007).

is the result of an expropriation or nationalization stipulated in Article III. In such types of conflicts, if the dispute cannot be resolved within one year, the investor can submit it to an ad hoc arbitral tribunal to settle in line with the Arbitration Rules of UNCITRAL.[61]

Some BITs have the narrow scope of application in the investor-state dispute settlement provisions. However, in recent years developed countries such as, USA has prepared a model BIT to address the broadest and detailed disputes definition. As an example, Article 24 of the US Model BIT provides that: "*1. In the event that a disputing party considers that an investment dispute cannot be settled by consultation and negotiation: (a) the claimant, on its own behalf, may submit to arbitration under this Section a claim (i) that the respondent has breached (A) an obligation under Articles 3 through 10, (B) an investment authorization, or (C) an investment agreement; and (ii) that the claimant has incurred loss or damage by reason of, or arising out of, that breach; and (b) the claimant, on behalf of an enterprise of the respondent that is a juridical person that the claimant owns or controls directly or indirectly, may submit to arbitration under this Section a claim (i) that the respondent has breached - 23 (A) an obligation under Articles 3 through 10, (B) an investment authorization, or (C) an investment agreement; and (ii) that the enterprise has incurred loss or damage by reason of, or arising out of, that breach,*"[62] Nevertheless, developing countries such as, Turkey has a model BIT which does not define disputes as in a detailed way as the USA. For example, Article VII of the Turkey Model BIT provides that "*1. Disputes between one of the Parties and an investor of the other Party, **in connection with his investment**, shall be notified in writing, including detailed information, by the investor to the recipient Party of the investment. As far as possible, the investor and the concerned Party shall endeavour to settle these disputes by consultations and negotiations in good faith.*"[63]

It is worth while to note that, the ambit of application of the investor-state dispute settlement mechanisms rely on both the specific provisions which are addressed this issue and related with the wording of the substantive treaty obligations.[64] Although

---

[61] UNCTAD op.cit., p. 103.
[62] USA BIT Model 2004, http://www.state.gov/documents/organization/38710.pdf, (visited 20.6.2007).
[63] Turkey Model BIT, Agreement Between the Republic of Turkey and ---------Concerning the Reciprocal Promotion and Protection of Investments,
http://www.unctad.org/sections/dite/iia/docs/Compendium//en/211%20volume%208.pdf (visited 20.6.2007)
[64] UNCTAD op.cit., p. 104.

the dispute settlement procedure restricts the disputes which deprives from the purported breach of the obligation according to the treaty, BITs might include different solutions that are related with the scope of this restriction.[65] In particular, "umbrella clauses" which can incorporate into the BIT probably will increase the security of the investor since these clauses are so broad that they can enclose nearly every possibility that an investor may faced with.[66]

B.   Legal Standing

The legal standing issue is quite uncomplicated in the investor-State dispute settlement procedures. The investor-state dispute settlement mechanisms are easily accessible for investors who invest in the country which is the territory of other contracting party to the BITs.[67] Therefore, it is clear that one contracting party's investor has a right which is called legal standing in arbitration procedures against other contracting party.

It is noteworthy that determining the nationality of the foreign investor is extremely important issue for a valid claim under a BIT since as mentioned above a BIT can be applicable only if the investor is a real person or a legal entity from one of the contracting states. In *Olguin v Paraguay* case the respondent asserted that the claimant did not have a right to submit its disputes under the Paraguay-Peru BIT since he has dual nationality and also is a resident in the United States. However, the tribunal refused this claim because in this case it would be irrelevant to apply Peruvian domestic law. Thus, the claimant was a Peruvian national and that was enough for claimant to rely on the Paraguay-Peru BIT.[68]

However the question might arise if a foreign company incorporates in the host country under the law of host country, could it be possible for the foreign investor to solve the dispute which is between itself and the host country according to the investor-State dispute settlement provisions. In fact, jurisdictional objections are mostly related with the nationality of the entity rather than a physical person. If one of these conditions is satisfied, the entity will be considered as a national of a State: "

---

[65] *Ibid.*

[66] See detailed informatiın at Seriki Hakeem, Umbrella Clauses and Investment Treaty Arbitration: All Encompassing or Respite for Sovereign States and State Entities, Journal of Business Law, 2007.

[67] Freyer Dana H., Garfinkel Barry H op.cit., p.76.

[68] See Decision on Jurisdiction (August 8, 2000) and Award (July 26, 2001) ICSID Case No. ARB/98/5. Mehren von M. George, Salomon T. Claudia, Navigating Through Investor-State Arbitrations an Overview of Bilateral Investment Treaty Claims, Dispute Resolution Journal, 2004, p. 71

a. It is incorporated in that State

b. It has its seat in that State or

c. It is controlled by investors from that State"[69]

As it is clearly seen that identifying the contracting party and the terms of "company" and "investor" are significantly important issues for investors and states. This is since so as to fall within the scope of a BIT, contracting company must qualify as an "investor" or "company" of a State party to that BIT. For example, Article 1(2) (b) of the Turkey-Sweden BIT defines "investor" to include "any legal person having its seat in the territory of either Contracting Party, or in a third country with a predominant interest of an investor of the other contracting party."[70] However, in order not to have any legal standing problem within the ICSID jurisdiction, the Turkey-Sweden BIT has also additional provision with respect to the definition of "legal person" who has a legal right to submit the investment dispute to proper dispute settlement mechanisms. Article 8 (2) of the Turkey-Sweden BIT provides: "For the purposes of this Article, any legal person which is constituted in accordance with the legislation of one contracting party and in which before a dispute arises the majority of shares are owned by investors of the other contracting party shall be treated in accordance with Article 25 (2) (b) of the said Washington Convention, as an investor of the other contracting party."[71]

Therefore, either a Swedish company or a Turkish company in which a Swedish company has investment should qualify as an "investor" under the Turkey-Sweden BIT with standing to request arbitration against Turkey.

C.   Preconditions for the Dispute Settlement Mechanism
a.   Consent

The parties should give consent to international arbitration because it is essential for ICSID's jurisdiction regarding an investment dispute.[72] The consent can be given by an investment agreement or treaty or national laws. In respect of BITs, the contracting parties should express their consent in the BIT so that they can submit their dispute to the international arbitration. There are various ways to grant their consent in the BIT, for example, in the Turkey-UK BIT Article 8 (2) provides that "*Each*

---

[69] *Ibid.* p.71-72.
[70] See Article 1(2) (b)of the Agreement Between the Kingdom of Sweden and the Republic of Turkey on the Reciprocal Promotion and Protection of Investments, http://www.unctad.org/sections/dite/iia/docs/bits/sweden_turkey.pdf (visited 20.6.2007).
[71] *Ibid.*
[72] Mehren & Salomon op.cit., p.74.

Contracting Party hereby consents submit to the International Centre for the Settlement of Investment Disputes (hereinafter referred to as "the Centre") for settlement by arbitration under the Convention on the Settlement of Investment Disputes between States and Nationals of other States, opened for signature at Washington on 18 March 1965 any legal dispute arising between that contracting party and a national or company of the other Contracting Party concerning an investment of the later in the territory of the former."[73] To rely on the jurisdiction of the international arbitration parties should mention their consent unambiguously but if the host country let the investor to submit the dispute to arbitration, the requirement will be fulfilled.[74]

b.   Exhaustion of Local Remedies

There is a serious question, which is whether the investor has to exhaust all of his rights or not in order to rely on the international arbitration in the investor-State dispute settlement procedure. This question has not an easy answer since priorities of the procedure have been changed considerably. In the past, exhaustion of the local remedies was deemed to be a necessary stage before claiming the case at the international level.   Scholars conceived international arbitration as an additional meaning of conflict resolution so that foreign investors could be allowed for utilizing international arbitration only if they did not manage the resolution of their dispute through the local jurisdiction of host country.[75] Therefore, 30 years ago, a group of BITs required the exhaustion of local remedies as a condition of resorting international arbitration. Nevertheless, this trend has changed recently.[76]

In the last 10 years, BITs have supported the idea that international arbitration is an alternative rather than an additional meaning of adjudication. Subsequently, the great numbers of these agreements do not include exhaustion of local remedies as a condition to utilize from the international arbitration provisions. However, with this method different techniques have begun to use especially in Turkey's BIT experience. Turkey signed many BITs with other countries which have different approaches for the exhausted local remedies.   For example, the BIT between Turkey and Romania reinforces exhaustion of local jurisdiction as a condition while Turkey-the USA BIT does not include any article about the exhaustion of local remedies for a priority to the

---

[73] See Article 8 (2) of the Agreement between the UK and Turkey.
[74] UNCTAD op.cit., p. 108.
[75] *Ibid.* p.108.
[76] *Ibid.* p.108.

application of the international arbitration. In fact Article 6 (4) of the Turkey-Romania BIT provides that *"In the event that the investment dispute cannot be resolved through the foreign procedures, the investor concerned is entitled to submit the dispute for conciliation or arbitration, to the International Centre for the Settlement of Investment Disputes, at any time after the exhaustion of domestic remedies or after the expiry of one year from the date when the dispute has been submitted by the concerned investor to the tribunals of the Contracting Party which is a party to the dispute and there has not been rendered a final award."*[77]

D.   The Forum of Arbitration

Recently, numerous investor-state dispute settlement provisions include article which refers to several existing international arbitration conventions in order to stipulate the rules which will be applied to the arbitral proceedings.[78] While previously signed BITs included both parties consent only ICSID arbitration, nowadays the more popular trend is granting rights to the foreign investor to choose another international arbitration forum. The main reason for this is, not all of the countries are signatory to the ICSID convention hence, this forum cannot be always available.

As we mentioned above the most common arbitration rules that prescribed in the BITs are ICSID and the ICSID Additional Facility Rules.[79] However, these rules can be applicable only if one of the parties is a member of the ICSID. In the other BITs, the Court of Arbitration of the International Chamber of Commerce (ICC) in Paris or the Arbitration Institute of the Chamber of Commerce of the Stockholm are chosen as a possible venues. Moreover, the chance of submitting the dispute to the ad hoc arbitration is also provided in the BITs. It is true that in many BITs, the most common rules chosen for ad hoc arbitration is Arbitration rules of the United Nations Commission on International Trade Law (UNCITRAL).

During the BIT negotiations several questions will arise between the contracting parties regarding the dispute resolution options: whether the investors have one or more option to choose the forum, or whether the possible options are exhaustive or not. [80]

---

[77] See Article 6(4) of the Agreement between Romaina and The Republic of Turkey on the Reciprocal Promotion and Protection of Investments.
http://www.unctad.org/sections/dite/iia/docs/bits/romania_turkey.pdf. (visited 20.6.2007).
[78] UNCTAD, Dispute Settlement: Investor-State op.cit., p.37.
[79] Ibid. p.42.
[80] UNCTAD op.cit., p. 110.

Contracting parties gave different responses for these questions and at the end of the negotiations; there might be different solutions for every BIT.

It should be noted that contracting parties mostly have chosen the trend which is providing more than one arbitration forum to adjudicate the dispute. In addition to this prevailing trend, most BITs provide options to chose different forum of arbitration exhaustively so that there will be no dispute about the venue of the arbitration. As an example, the model BIT of Turkey provides such a regulation at the Article VII (2) which is about settlement of disputes between one party and investors of the other party. It points out that "*2. If these disputes, cannot be settled in this way within six months following the date of the written notification mentioned in paragraph 1, the dispute can be submitted, as the investor may choose, to:*

(a) the International Center for Settlement of Investment Disputes (ICSID) set up by the " Convention on Settlement of Investment Disputes Between States and Nationals of other States", in case both Parties become signatories of this Convention,

(b) an ad hoc court of arbitration laid down under the Arbitration Rules of Procedure of the United Nations Commission for International Trade Law (UNCITRAL)."[81]

Although Turkey has such a model BIT, still most of the BITs that it had signed before, include settling of investment disputes only with regard to ICSID rules. For instance, Article 8 (2) of the Netherlands-Turkey BIT provides that " *(...) If the dispute cannot be resolved through the foregoing procedures the investor concerned may choose to submit the dispute to the International Centre for the Settlement of Investment Disputes ('Centre') for settlement by arbitration, at any time after one year from the date upon which the dispute arose provided that in case the investor concerned has brought the dispute before the courts of justice of the Contracting Country that is a party to the dispute, and there has not been rendered a final award.*"[82]

The more recent and popular method utilized in BITs is permitting the investor to choose the specific arbitration forum in which the case will be adjudicated. In fact, BITs provide certainty to contracting parties about the forum where the dispute will be settled with this new approach. It should be worth while to note that when providing the right of choosing the arbitration venue to the investor, host countries seek to satisfy investors and give confidence in order to make them invest in their countries.

---

[81] See Article VII (2) of the Turkey Model BIT.
[82] See Article 8 (2) of the Netherlands-Turkey BIT.

E. Applicable Law

In a traditional way, some of the BITs include provisions with regard to applicable substantive law for disputes between investor and state. This could be true but in most applicable law provisions of the BITs are drafted broadly and as much as generally it can be. Parties do not seek to be so specific about this issue in the BIT. In my opinion notably host country does not prefer making specific provisions about the governing law since if the host country specifies the applicable law, investors may not seek to invest in that country. Hence, both of the parties wish to take the advantage of broad governing law provision so that possible disputes can be solved according to the circumstances and the discretion of the tribunal. For example, Article 8 (4) of the Turkey-Lebanese BIT states that "The arbitral tribunal shall decide the dispute in accordance with the provisions of this Agreement, the applicable rules and principles of International law, and the national law when applicable..."[83]

As we mentioned above, the determination of the governing law depends on the circumstances of the dispute, the choice of law provisions and the applicable arbitration rules. International arbitration rules such as, ICDR[84] and ICC[85] provide that if the parties can not agree on the point of the applicable law, the tribunal will have to utilize its authority of discretion to decide which law will be applicable for the dispute. In addition to this, the governing law that will be decided by the tribunal should be the most appropriate with regard to the situation. [86] Article 33 of the UNICITRAL rules also provide that when the parties failed to indicate the law to be applied, the tribunal will apply the law determined by the conflict law rules which it considers appropriate.[87]

In addition to these ICSID also has similar provision which is regulated in the article 42 (1): "in the absence of the agreement between the parties with respect to the choice of law, the tribunal shall apply the law of the host country and such rules of international arbitration as be applicable."

---

[83] See Article 8 (4) of the Agreement between the Lebanese Republic and the Republic of Turkey on the Promotion and Reciprocal Protection of Investments,
http://www.unctad.org/sections/dite/iia/docs/bits/lebanon_turkey.pdf (visited 20.6.2007).
[84] Article 28 of the Rules of International Centre for Dispute Resolution (ICDR), www.adr.org (visited 16.7.2007).
[85] Article 17 of the Rules of Arbitration of the International Chamber of Commerce (ICC),
http://www.iccwbo.org/court/english/arbitration/rules.asp (visited 16.7.2007).
[86] Mehren & Salomon op.cit., p.73.
[87] UNCITRAL Arbitration Rules, http://www.uncitral.org/pdf/english/texts/arbitration/arb-rules/arb-rules.pdf (visited 16.7.2007).

F.   Enforcement of the Arbitral Awards

Like in the past, most recent BITs stipulate that "an award shall be final and binding for the parties to the dispute". Therefore, the parties are not allowed to resubmit their dispute for adjudication if one of the parties is not satisfied with the final judgement. If once the arbitral award is rendered in an investor-state proceeding, the decision will be binding, final and enforceable. However, countries have no obligation about recognizing and enforcing the award that is made outside their domestic jurisdictions, except an international convention provides the recognition and enforcement of an arbitral award. It can be said that most of international agreements oblige their members to enforce and recognise an arbitral award under certain circumstances in their national jurisdictions. There are two main international treaties for the recognition and enforcement of arbitral awards first is the ICSID convention second is the United Nations Convention on the Recognition and Enforcement of Foreign Arbitral Awards which was signed in New York 1958.[88] We will explain the enforcement and recognition of ICSID award at the next chapter in more detail.

It would be worth while to note that most of BITs include articles which aim to regulate the enforcement and recognition of arbitral awards. For example, Article VII (4) of the Turkey-Algeria BIT provides that "The arbitration awards shall be final and binding for all parties in dispute. Each party commits itself to execute the award according to its national law."[89]

III.   Recent Developments on Investor-State Dispute Settlement Procedures
A.   General Improvements in Investor-State Dispute Settlement Procedures

The recent ICSID and other institutional and ad hoc arbitral decisions have affected the evolution of dispute settlement procedures under BITs. In fact, some countries such as USA and Canada have started to incorporate new issues in investor-state dispute settlement provisions of BITs. As explained before, most BITs have one article regarding investor-state dispute settlement procedures. However, the new trend for BITs shows that the recent BITs include comprehensive and detailed provisions and

---

[88] UNCTAD op.cit., p. 116.
[89] See Article VII (4).of the Agreement the Government of the Republic of Turkey and the Government of the Democratic and Popular Republic of Algeria Concerning the Reciprocal Promotion and Protection of Investments, http://www.unctad.org/sections/dite/iia/docs/bits/turkey_algeria.pdf (visited 20.6.2007).

even one chapter for this procedure. In particular, some BITs of Canada, Austria, Mexico and the United States follow this trend.

It is worthwhile to note that the followings are the main aims of this new trend in investor-state dispute settlement procedures: "to promote great predictability and contracting parties control over arbitration", " to promote judicial economy", " to promote consistent jurisprudence on international investment law" and to promote transparency of arbitration proceedings.[90] To carry out these objectives, some BITs provide detailed and specific investor-state dispute settlement provisions.

Some BITs follow the NAFTA's investment chapter which addressed issues that traditionally most BITs do not cover, such as preliminary objections, measures for interim injunctive relief and specifying the place of arbitration.[91] Furthermore, in order to avoid "frivolous claims", some BITs include provisions that provide expedited procedure. For example Article 28 of the United States-Uruguay BIT set out expedited procedure through regulating preliminary stage and specific time frames.[92]

There are some BITs that provide limitation to one arbitration forum in order to promote judicial economy. Pursuant to these treaties, if an investor chooses to recourse a claim to domestic courts, he can lose the right to arbitration. This situation is called as a "fork in the road" provision. Article 8 (3) of The Chile and Egypt BIT illustrates this approach: " Once the investor has submitted the dispute to the competent tribunal of the Contracting Party in whose territory the investment was made or to international arbitration, that election shall be final."[93]

B. Creating an Appeal Mechanism

Even though the finality of arbitration proceedings is one of the main advantages of international arbitration, some scholars argue that there should be an appeal for investment disputes[94] The main reason of their argument is that there might be some inconsistent awards on the same questions or facts. The *CME v Czech Republic*[95] and

---

[90] UNCTAD op.cit., p.119.
[91] *Ibid.* p.120.
[92] UNCTAD, Investor-State Disputes Arising From Investment Treaties: A Review, 2005, p.56.
[93] See Article 8 (3) of the Agreement between the Government of the Arab Republic of Egypt and the Government of the Republic of Chile on the Reciprocal Promotion and Protection of Investments, http://www.unctad.org/sections/dite/iia/docs/bits/chile_egypt.pdf (Visited 23.8.2007).
[94] Yannaca-Small Katia , Improving the System of Investor-State Dispute Settlement: An Overview, OECD Working Papers on International Investment, Number 2006/1., paragraph 27.
[95] CME Czech Republic B. V. v. Czech Republic Partial Award (September 13, 2001), Ibid. footnote 28.

Lauder v Czech Republic [96]are two examples of inconsistent decisions rendered by ICSID Tribunal based on the same or similar facts. Some countries have recently concluded BITs which include an appeal mechanism for investment disputes.[97] However, there might be some consequences and problems of creation an appeal mechanism. In particular, the problem will occur between the appellate mechanism and the existing international arbitration conventions.

C.   Transparency in Investor-State Dispute Settlement Procedure

The transparency is an essential issue in investor-state dispute settlement procedures since investor-state disputes often raise public interest issues which are not so common in international commercial arbitration.[98] Some BITs which are influence mainly from the Chapter 11 of the NAFTA include transparency provisions. However, incorporating the transparency provisions into the BITs is not practical and effective in arbitration proceedings, thus in particular international arbitration rules should provide transparency, in order to do that these rules should be amended.[99] In fact, ICSID rules are amended to provide effective and efficient transparency in investor-state dispute settlement procedure. Moreover, transparency could be improved by a requirement for the publication of all notices of arbitration under any investor-state dispute settlement mechanism. In fact, recent BITs signed by United States provide this issue and the ICSID is also publicised the names of the parties, subject of the case and its procedural stages. It should be noted that the transparency should be provided not only for the arbitration proceedings, but also the arbitral awards.

---

[96] Lauder v.Czech Republic (Final Award) (September 3, 2002), Ibid, footnote 29.
[97] UNCTAD Bilateral Investment Treaties 1995-2006: Trends In Investment Rule Making op cit., p.123.
[98] Legum Barton, Investment Treaty Arbitration's Contribution To International Commercial Arbitration, Dispute Resolution Journal, August-October, 2005 p.73-74; OECD Investment Committee, Transparency and Third Party Participation in Investor-State Dispute Settlement Procedures, Working Papers on International Investment, Number 2005/1, paragraph 1.
[99] UNCTAD, Investor-State Disputes Arising From Investment Treaties: A Review, 2005, p.56.

CHAPTER 3   Main Features of ICSID Arbitration

I.   Overview of ICSID

As explained in Chapter 1, the establishment of ICSID is the main step for the development of arbitration in international investment disputes since the ICSID Convention which was drafted in the framework of the World Bank focused on the settlement of investment disputes. Moreover, the ICSID Convention is extensively ratified by developed as well as developing countries and the utilizing the arbitration mechanism under the ICSID Convention is also common.

It is true that ICSID administers conciliation and arbitration process, but ICSID does not carry out them.[100] This mission is left to the Conciliation Commission or Arbitral Tribunal whose members come from panels that ICSID maintains with regard to the Convention. When the parties reach an agreement, they can select the conciliators or the arbitrators but the numbers of conciliators or arbitrators must be odd. If parties cannot agree, the Convention provides that the number of conciliators or arbitrators should be three.[101] Each party chooses one arbitrator or conciliator and after this both of the parties have to agree the third one who will be the president of the tribunal.[102] After the arbitration proceedings, the Arbitral Tribunal can decide an award by majority and this award is binding for both of the parties and is also enforceable.[103]

II.   Benefits of the ICSID Convention

As we mentioned in Chapter 1, the main goal of the ICSID is facilitating the private international investment by the creation of a preferable investment climate. In order to fulfil this aim, the ICSID convention grants some benefits both to foreign investors and host states. The benefit for investors is gaining the access to the efficient international forum when a dispute arises. Going to arbitration is very important for legal security since it is required for an investment decision.[104] The host state's advantages are; firstly by giving the opportunity of arbitration host state enhances its

---

[100] UNCTAD, Course on Dispute Settlement International Centre For Settlement of Investment Disputes, (2.1 Overview), United Nations, New York and Geneva, 2003, p.9; Sureda Andres Rigo, Two Views on ICSID Arbitration, World Arbitration and Mediation Report, June 2002, p.166.
[101] See Article 37 of the ICSID Convention, ICSID, ICSID Convention, Regulations and Rules, http://www.worldbank.org/icsid/basicdoc/intro.htm (visited 05.05.2007)
[102] Lopina A. David, The International Centre For Settlement of Investment Disputes: Investment Arbitration for the 1990s., Ohio State Journal on Dispute Resolution, 1988, p 110.
[103] UNCTAD, 2.1 Overview, op.cit., p 13.
[104] *Ibid*, p.13.

investment climate.[105] Thus, it can catch the attention of more foreign investors so that attract more international investment. Secondly, host state could also shield itself against other kinds of foreign or international litigation by giving consent to ICSID arbitration[106]. Furthermore, host state can also protect itself against diplomatic protection which is granted to foreign investors.[107]

III. Jurisdiction of the ICSID Convention

Article 25 (1) of the Convention stipulates three preconditions which are personal jurisdiction, consent of the parties and subject matter of jurisdiction for the ICSID's jurisdiction.

A. Personal Jurisdiction

Article 25 mentions only one condition for investor who has to be "a national of another contracting state".[108] This leads to an exclusion of jurisdiction over disputes which are between states or disputes between state and its own national. As it is known almost all of the investors are corporations, so the issue of nationality is defined by the location of incorporation or the place of the head office.[109] Joint ventures are the main types of investments and they incorporated mostly in host country so if nationality requirement is applied in this situation, ICSID arbitration would be excluded.[110] Article 25 (2) (b) of the Convention has produced a solution for this problem. According to Article 25 (2) (b) when parties agree to treat the company which is incorporated locally as if it is a national of other state, there will be no problem with regard to ICSID arbitration.[111] It is true that this approach provides the Convention enhanced its scope of application.

It should be noted that as explained previous chapter, drafting clear arbitration clause is important for solving above mentioned problem. In the ICSID arbitration *Holiday Inns/Occidental Petroleum v. Government of Morocco*, the tribunal held that the agreement between contracting parties about foreign nationality of the locally

---

[105] *Ibid*, p.13.
[106] *Ibid*. p.13.
[107] *Ibid*, p 12.
[108] See Article 25 of the ICSID Convention.
[109] Wolfgang Peter, Arbitration and Renegotiation of International Investment Agreements, Martinus Nijhoff Publishers, 1986, p 205.
[110] *Ibid*.
[111] Lobina op.cit., p.113.

incorporated company must be precise since the Article 25 (2) (b) is the exception of the general rule which is the investor must be different nationality from the host state.[112]

B.   Consent

It should be noted that to be a member of the ICSID Convention does not enough for the ICSID Jurisdiction. For the existence of the jurisdiction, the ICSID convention demands separate written consents from contracting parties.[113] There are several ways to give consent to the Centre's jurisdiction. It can be given in a direct agreement between host state and investor like a concession contract. Also consent may be given by a "standing offer" from the host state to investor and when the investor accepted it in appropriate fashion, the consent will be legally proper.[114] This standing offer can be included in the host state's legislation and standing offer might also be designated in the treaty which is signed between host state's and investor's state of nationality. Numerous BITs and Energy Charter Treaty provide such standing offers.[115]

It is seen clearly from the cases of the ICSID arbitration that the trend of consent through direct agreement between parties has changed to grant consent by a general offer from the host state which is often acknowledged by the investor through instituting proceedings.[116] The consent that is given by both of the parties separately to arbitration under the convention is binding. Thus, it cannot be annulled unilaterally, once it is given by both parties.[117] It is important to mention that when the parties grant consent, they may set the consent with regard to some conditions or limitations. For example, host states might apply to ICSID jurisdiction only with regard to certain kinds of disputes such as, questions regarding compensation for expropriation.[118] Consent also can be given as a condition on certain procedural steps for example, previous attempt to settle the dispute.[119]

---

[112] Wolfgang Peter op.cit., p 205.
[113] UNCTAD, Course on Dispute Settlement International Centre For Settlement of Investment Disputes, (2.3. Consent to Arbitration), United Nations, New York and Geneva, 2003, p.5.
[114] UNCTAD, 2.1 Overview op.cit., p 16.
[115] UNCTAD, 2.3. Consent to Arbitration op.cit., p.6
[116] UNCTAD, 2.1 Overview op.cit., p 16.
[117] See Article 25 of the ICSID Convention.
[118] UNCTAD, 2.3. Consent to Arbitration op.cit., p.29-30.
[119] UNCTAD, 2.1 Overview op.cit., p 16.

C.   Subject Matter of Jurisdiction

The subject matter of jurisdiction of ICSID is defined at article 25 of the ICSID Convention: "Any legal dispute arising directly out of an investment."[120] Thus, ICSID's subject matter jurisdiction has three elements:

1.   The dispute must be legal.

2.   The dispute must arise directly out of underlying transaction.

3.   Such underlying transaction must qualify as an investment.

Firstly, the legal dispute requirement for ICSID jurisdiction is an easy requirement to meet. The report of the Executive Directors states that the disputes "must concern the existence or scope of a legal right or obligation, or the nature or extent of the reparation to be made for breach of a legal obligation."[121] In arbitration practice almost every claim is formulated in terms of a legal right or obligation.

Secondly, the requirement of directness reflects the aim of the Convention since the ICSID was established for the promotion of foreign investment and the encouragement of international investment. A dispute must be "reasonably, closely connected" to an investment in order to meet the requirement of directness.[122]

Thirdly, the definition of investment is the vital to the ICSID Convention's subject matter jurisdiction. However, the ICSID Convention does not include a definition of the term investment. There were so many oppositions to include definition of investment in the Convention but the main reason for not incorporating the definition of investment in the Convention is to avoid lengthy jurisdictional discussions.[123] Thus, the Convention grants parties to have wide discretion rights to describe their transactions as an investment. However, the parties do not have unrestricted freedom in determination of investment since pursuant to Article 41 of the Convention a tribunal may examine on its own motion whether the requirements of jurisdiction are met.[124] In addition, even there is no precise definition in the ICSID Convention, the arbitral tribunal look for typical features of investments under the Convention. For example, "certain duration of the relevant activities, the regularity of profit and return, the presences of a certain economic risk, and a substantial commitment as well as the

---

[120] See Article 25 of the ICSID Convention.
[121] UNCTAD, Course on Dispute Settlement International Centre For Settlement of Investment Disputes, (2.5. Requirements Ratione Materiae), United Nations, New York and Geneva, 2003, p.9.
[122] Ibid. p.12.
[123] Lobina op.cit., p.114.
[124] See Article 41 of the ICSID Convention.

relevance of the project for the host state's development"[125] are typical features to identify the definition of investment under the Convention.

As mentioned above the parties can describe their transaction as an investment in an agreement with explicitly or implicitly. In particular, as explained in chapter two many BITs include a provision to explain what the investment is (definition of investment). It should be also noted that the concept of investment has been interpreted broadly in arbitration practice.[126]

IV. Three Characteristics of ICSID Arbitration

It is true that there are three characteristics of ICSID Arbitration which differentiate ICSID arbitration from other forms of international commercial arbitration. Firstly, the law which can be applicable to substance of the dispute is one difference. Secondly, ICSID arbitration limits the role on the national courts in the arbitral procedure. Thirdly, ICSID Convention provides an effective system of enforcement of ICSID award.

A. Applicable Law

ICSID convention has not any substantive rules. It provides a procedure for the settlement of investment disputes. The reason for this is the thought of trying to clarify the substantive law of international investment in the framework of the Convention would have caused to insuperable problems.[127]

However, ICSID Convention includes an article about applicable law. Article 42 of the ICSID Convention provides contracting parties have the freedom of choosing the law that will be applied to their disputes.[128] By giving this right to the parties, Article 42 shows its respect to the party autonomy. The parties can choose the law of the State that is one of the parties or the State of which investor is a national, or it can be the law of a third country where has no connection with the parties. If the parties decided to utilize such a right, the tribunal had to respect this and must apply the chosen law. In addition to this, parties might agree that the tribunal may decide the dispute *ex aequo et bono*. There are some situations that constitute an excess to the tribunal's

---

[125] UNCTAD, (2.1. Overview) op.cit., p.14.
[126] *Ibid.*
[127] *Ibid.* p 14.
[128] See Article 42 of the ICSID Convention.

authority and lead to the annulment of the award.[129] These are the failure of application of rules, or chosen law by parties, or if no choice is made, the application of default provisions of Article 42 (1). If the claim is brought according to the provisions of any BITs, the rules of chosen law for the aim of Article 42 will be those provided in the agreement under international law.[130] If parties do not choose any law, Article 42 (1) provides the solution for this situation by stating the application of host state law "(including its rules on the conflict of laws) and such rules of international law as may be applicable."[131]

If there is an absence of agreement on the applicable law, the tribunal is required to apply the law of the host state. In addition, the provision includes a *renvoi* provision in order to alleviate the reference to the law of the host state.[132] If there is a reference to the international law, this means that this reference is to all of the sources of international law which is referred to in Article 38 of the Statute of the International Court of Justice.[133] ICSID tribunals adopted several versions of the role of international law but the popular trend is for international law, it must play additional or complementary role in order to fill the gaps or corrective role to provide the harmony when the host state's law does not conform with the international law.[134] However, if the host state law is in violation of a mandatory rule of international law, an ICSID Tribunal may not decide the award on the basis of host state's law.[135] International law might also be applicable if chosen law is host states law and the law can make the international law directly applicable to the dispute.[136]

B.   Arbitration Procedure

The second discrepancy that separates ICSID arbitration from other types of arbitration is the self-contained nature of the ICSID arbitration procedure.[137] If the arbitration takes place according to the provisions of the ICSID Convention, the

---

[129] See Article 52 of the ICSID Convention.
[130] Collins Lawrence, Morse C G J, McClean David, Briggs Adrian, Harris Jonathan, McLachlan Campbell op cit., p 781.
[131] See Article 42 (1) of the ICSID Convention.
[132] UNCTAD, Course on Dispute Settlement International Centre For Settlement of Investment Disputes, (2.5.Applicable law), United Nations, New York and Geneva, 2003, p.18
[133] Collins Lawrence, Morse C G J, McClean David, Briggs Adrian, Harris Jonathan, McLachlan Campbell op.cit., p 783.
[134] *Ibid.* p.782.
[135] UNCTAD, 2.5.Applicable law op.cit., p.25.
[136] *Ibid.*
[137] Collins Lawrence, Morse C G J, McClean David, Briggs Adrian, Harris Jonathan, McLachlan Campbell op.cit., p 782.

arbitration procedure is self-contained and insulated from interference of the national courts. This situation is a contrast with the situation of the arbitrations that are directed from the outside of the ICSID with regard to BIT and also with the situation which the tribunal is established according to ICSID's Additional Facility.[138]

It is important to note that the *lex arbitri* of the ICSID arbitration is specially "ICSID Convention and the ICSID arbitration rules and not the law of the seat of the arbitration".[139] The Convention includes an internal annulment procedure which is unique for its own.[140] It made an exclusion that is the right of recourse to the national courts. Provisional measures can only be sought from ICSID tribunal and not by national courts but if the parties agree, provisional measures can sought from national courts.[141]

C.   Enforcement

If investor has submitted an investor-state dispute to the national court in a host country, at this situation there will be no special problems regarding enforcement. Since the national court that held the judgment has the ability of enforce that judgment. However, when investor-state dispute has submitted to the international arbitration, particular issues of enforcement may arise. For example, an investor usually seeks to have the full content of arbitral award enforced although the tribunal will not have the final means of enforcement that is available for the domestic courts.[142] Article 54 (1) mentions this thought and clarifies the problem by stating that *"Each Contracting State shall recognise an award rendered pursuant to this Convention as binding and enforce the pecuniary obligations imposed by that award within its territories as if it were a final judgement of a courting that State... "[143]*

The main issue which is understood from this provision is that when an investor-state dispute is held pursuant to the ICSID arbitration, each State where a party to the Convention must enforce the resulting arbitral award in its territory.[144] Nevertheless, in

---

[138] *Ibid.* p.783.
[139] *Ibid.* p 783.
[140] See Article 52 of the ICSID Convention.
[141] Collins Lawrence, Morse C G J, McClean David, Briggs Adrian, Harris Jonathan, McLachlan Campbell op.cit., p 783.
[142] UNCTAD, Dispute Setlement: Investor-State op.cit.,p.62.
[143] *Ibid.* p.62.
[144] Nmehielle Vincent O. Orlu, Enforcing Arbitration Awards Under the International Convention For the Settlement of Investment Disputes (ICSID Convention), Annual Survey of International and Comparative Law, Spring 2001, p.30.

some particular situations, a party to the ICSID Convention cannot fulfil the enforcement for the reason of the interaction between the provisions of Article 54 and Article 55. In particular, Article 55 provides reservation of that country's municipal law on sovereign immunity against execution.[145] There is a sample case about this situation which is held in a case from the District Court. The decision of the District Court is for the Southern District of New York in *LETCO v. Liberia* which the court depended on the Article 55 and held that "certain Liberian property was immune from execution."[146]

Moreover, according to the Article 54 (1) the pecuniary obligations are imposed by the award can be enforceable. Thus, non-pecuniary obligations imposed by the award are left outside the limit of enforcement. There are so many examples that can be given to non-pecuniary obligations such as, "the reinstatement of wrongfully discharged personnel or compliance with performance requirements like the use of local components"[147]. The certain situations which can be non-pecuniary obligations imposed by the award could be "the restitution of seized property and the granting of a permission to transfer currency".[148] It is extremely important to note that obligations that are not expressed as monetary terms imposed by the award are also binding, even if with regard to Article 54 these obligations are not enforceable.

V.   Recent Amendments to the ICSID Arbitration Rules

ICSID recently amended its rules of procedure for arbitration proceedings on April 10, 2006.[149] Since, the number of investor-state dispute arbitrations has increased and as we explained in previous chapter, there were new developments on BITs. The recent amendments to ICSID arbitration rules are the result of negotiations and consultations with the non-governmental organisations, governments, arbitration experts and legal scholars.[150] It is essential to note that the main aim of these amendments is to improve the ICSID arbitration process. In particular, the following issues are the main

---

[145] *Ibid.* p.31.
[146] UNCTAD, Dispute Setlement: Investor-State op.cit., p.62.
[147] UNCTAD, Course on Dispute Settlement International Centre For Settlement of Investment Disputes, (2.9 Binding Force and Enforcement), p.14.
[148] *Ibid.*
[149] ICSID, ICSID Convention, Regulations and Rules, Introduction, http://www.worldbank.org/icsid/basicdoc/intro.htm (visited 05.05.2007)
[150] Finizio Steven P, Mortensen Julian Davis, Shenkman Ethan G, Recent Developments in Investor-State Arbitration: Effective Use of Provisional Measures, The European Arbitration Review, p.2. http://www.globalarbitrationreview.com/handbooks/3/sections/5/chapters/31/recent-developments-investor-state-arbitration-effective-use-provisional-measures (visited 05.05.2007)

amendments[151]: 1. Third party participation, 2. Publication of awards, 3. Preliminary procedures, 4. Arbitrators disclosure requirements.

1. Third Party Participation

The question has been arisen as to whether non-parties should be allowed to make amicus curiae submissions in investment arbitrations. Amicus curiae can be defined "a person who is not a party to a law suit but who petitions the courts or is requested by the court to file a brief in the action because that person has a strong interest in the subject matter."[152] Amicus curiae submissions let the public interests groups to intervene the ICSID arbitration proceedings.[153] Pursuant to new r. 37 of ICSID arbitration rules amicus curiae submissions are accepted in certain conditions by the ICSID tribunal.[154] According to this article the tribunal has a right to decide whether to allow amicus curiae submission or not. Even though parties have a right to consultation regarding amicus curiae briefs, they do not have a veto right.[155] This amendment empowers arbitration tribunals to allow amicus curiae submissions by non-parties with an interest in an investment dispute. In addition, this amendment increases transparency through acceptance of non-parties submissions.

2. Publication of Awards

The amendments made to ICSID arbitration rules requires publication of awards. r. 48 of the ICSID arbitration rules provides that "the centre shall, however, promptly include in its publication excerpts of the legal reasoning of the tribunal."[156] This amendment requires publication of ICSID awards and excerpts of the legal rules applied by the tribunal.[157] Thus, the ICSID awards and its legal reasoning can be easily accessible to the public. As we explained in the chapter two, transparency issue has been considered in recent signed BITs. These new amendment provides transparency through requiring publication of awards.

---

[151] Caruba Sandra L. Op.cit., p.149.

[152] Black's Law Dictionary, 8 th Edition, Thomson West, 2004, p.93.

[153] Santens Ank, ICSID Amends Its Arbitration Rules, International Arbitration Law Review, 2006, p.120.

[154] See Rule 37 of the ICSID Rules of Procedure for Arbitration Proceedings (Arbitration Rules), ICSID Convention, Regulations and Rules, http://www.worldbank.org/icsid/basicdoc/basicdoc.htm (visited 05.05.2007).

[155] Santens Ank op.cit., p.120.

[156] Rule 48 of the ICSID Rules of Procedure for Arbitration Proceedings (Arbitration Rules).

[157] Santens Ank op.cit., p.120.

3.   Preliminary Procedures

r. 39 of the ICSID arbitration rules allows a party to request provisional measures "at any time after the institution of the proceedings".[158] The aim of this amendment is to improve a tribunal's ability to grant provisional measures on an expedited basis. Pursuant to r. 39 a party may request for provisional measures even before the tribunal constituted. However, the tribunal still has the power to decide on such a request. In addition, the amendments require the ICSID Secretary General to draft a briefing schedule so that the provisional measure can be promptly considered by the tribunal as soon as it is formed.[159] However, even with these amendments the procedure governing for provisional measures may still take time so parties can seek provisional measures form national court. It should be noted that in order to allow preliminary objections to frivolous claims ICSID amended its rules. In fact r. 41 of the ICSID arbitration rule provides that a party has a preliminary objection right if the claim is "manifestly without legal merit". Thus, the amendments create a fast-track procedure to object the claims which are obviously without legal merit.[160]

4.   Arbitrators Disclosure Requirements

r.6 of the ICSID arbitration rules requires each arbitrator to sign a declaration of independence.[161] The new amendment of this rule explicitly provides that disclosers should include any circumstances which may affect the arbitrator's independence.[162]

Overall, the ICSID amendments may improve the ICSID arbitration process in particular, providing transparency through allowing third party participation and publication of awards. The effectiveness of these amendments is going to be seen after their application and implication in the investment arbitration proceedings. It is worth while to note that the proposed amendments included an appeal mechanism within ICSID. However, this proposal was not accepted.[163] As we analysed in previous chapter, the recent BITs include an appeal mechanism for investment disputes. Thus, in the future the ICSID arbitration rules will probably be amended to incorporate an appeal mechanism within ICSID.

---

[158] See Rule 39 of the ICSID Rules of Procedure for Arbitration Proceedings (Arbitration Rules).
[159] Finizio Steven P, Mortensen Julian Davis, Shenkman Ethan G, op.cit., p.3.
[160] Santens Ank op.cit., p.121.
[161] see Rule 6 of the ICSID Rules of Procedure for Arbitration Proceedings (Arbitration Rules).
[162] Santens Ank op.cit., p.121.
[163] *Ibid.* p.122.

CHAPTER 4   ICSID Cases Against Turkey Regarding Energy Sector

I.   Concluded Case: PSEG Global Inc v. Turkey

The recently concluded ICSID case against Turkey is an important award for effecting Turkish energy sector and determines the essential role of bilateral investment treaties on investor-state dispute settlement mechanism. As this dissertation analyzed the main requirements of investor-state dispute settlement mechanism and in particular, ICSID in previous chapters, the PSEG v Turkey case illustrates the same issues in a practical aspects. Thus, this case is a good example of showing the development of international arbitration on investment disputes.

On May 2, 2002, ICSID registered a request for arbitration against the Republic of Turkey ("Turkey" or "Respondent") from PSEG Global Inc. (PSEG), a USA Company; the North American Coal Corporation (North American Coal), a USA Company; and Konya Ilgin Elektrik Üretim ve Ticaret Limited Şirketi (the "Project Company"). ICSID arbitration was provided for in bilateral investment treaty signed between USA and Turkey in 1985 and which entered into force in 1990.[164]

A.   The Facts of the Dispute

Turkey has needed to expand its energy sector since 1980s so as to ensure the development of its economy. Thus, Turkey launched its energy expansion program. Within this program, Turkish Parliament enacted and revamped many laws to promote and protect national and foreign investors' investment on energy sector. For example, Turkish Parliament enacted Law No. 3096 allowing private companies to build and operate generation facilities and to sell the generated electricity to TEAS, the Turkish state owned electricity entity.[165] The Build-Operate-Transfer (BOT) model was established in accordance with this Law.

Foreign investors are the key elements of Turkish energy expansion program. Indeed, like other foreign investors, PSEG, started negotiations of a contract with the Turkish Ministry of Energy to develop a lignite-fired electric power plant in the Turkish Province of Konya in April 1994. However, these negotiations were delayed by bureaucratic measures that culminated in the termination of the investment project in

---

[164] See Turkey-USA BIT.
[165] PSEG Global Inc., The North American Coal Corporation, and Konya Ilgın Elektrik Üretim ve Ticaret Limited Şirketi (CLAIMANT) and Republic of Turkey (Respondent), <u>Decision on Jurisdiction,</u> ICSID Case No. ARB/02/5, Paragraph 18.

January 2000 by the Turkish administration after seven years of ineffective negotiations.

The following issues are the disputed issues between the parties: whether the Contract was an investment, whether it was legal and binding, and whether it included a final agreement on key commercial terms, etc.

Before analyzing the merits of the case, it is important to explain the jurisdiction issues of this case. In fact, this dissertation examines the investor-state dispute settlement mechanism provided under bilateral investment treaties. Thus, the jurisdictional aspects of this case is an essential for this study to show the practical aspects of the main requirements of investor-state dispute settlement procedure, such as "the definition of investment and investment disputes" and " legal standing" etc.

B. Jurisdictional Issues

Turkey challenged the Tribunal's jurisdiction on the following grounds:

a. There is no investment or an investment dispute under the ICSID Convention or USA-Turkey BIT,

b. Suppose that there was an investment, Turkey has not consented to Jurisdiction,

c. The requirements under USA-Turkey BIT to submit to any previously agreed dispute settlement procedure has not been met,

d. The North American Coal Corporation and the Project Company do not have legal standing in this case.[166]

It is essential to examine these reasons briefly since in the previous chapters, this dissertation analyzed the similar issues and we argue that the drafters of the BITs should be careful in the wording of the treaties.

1. Definition of Investment

Turkey argued that USA-Turkey BIT protection extends only to the investment defined in the Article I of the BIT and the proposed project and concession contract are not an investment under this article.[167] Turkey asserted that even though the Contract was signed there was no agreement on commercial terms due to the Claimant's underestimation of project costs. Therefore, the activities were undertaken by the PSEG were only preparatory to the investment and there was no legally binding investment

---

[166] *Ibid.* Paragraph 61.
[167] *Ibid.* Paragraph 66.

project at all. Turkey also argued that there was "no meeting of the minds" on the Contract was approved by the Turkish authorities.[168] Thus, there in no investment under the BIT, so the Tribunal has lack of jurisdiction.

Conversely, PSEG argued that Turkey breached its various contractual undertakings. Claimant contended that there is a legally valid and binding contract between the parties. In order to support its arguments, among other things, the Claimant cited the UNIDROIT Principles of International Commercial Contracts stating that "it is not always necessary to reach an agreement on all the essential terms of a contract as long as the parties have the intention of forming a contract"[169]

The Tribunal firstly concluded that the Concession Contract exist since it was duly signed and approved by Turkish authorities. However, the essential dispute between the parties is whether the contract valid or not. In paragraph 96 of the Award, the Tribunal stated, *"There are, however, other documents which the Tribunal believes are particularly important in establishing the intent of the parties to conclude and be bound by the Contract. The most fundamental of these is evidently the Contract itself. There are many provisions in the Contract which evidence the intent of the parties to be bound."*[170] Thus, the Tribunal found that the concession contract exists and is valid and legally binding. This is enough to establish that "the Tribunal has jurisdiction on the basis of an investment having made in the form of a Concession Contract."[171] As we analyzed in Chapter 2, the broad "investment" definition were embodied in numerous bilateral investment treaties. The Tribunal in this case rightly decided that the Concession Contract constitutes investment which is stipulated in Article I (1) (c) of the USA-Turkey BIT.[172]

2.   Definition of Investment Dispute

Turkey also argued that even if there is an investment, the dispute did not arise out of an investment in the meaning of Article 25 of the ICSID Convention. As already mentioned in previous chapter, the ICSID Convention did not define the "investment dispute". Thus, national laws and generally bilateral investment treaties define the "investment dispute" in a great detail. According to the Article VI (1) of the USA-

---

[168] *Ibid.* Paragraph 67-73.
[169] UNIDROIT Principles of International Commercial Contracts, 1994, Article 2.14.
[170] *Ibid.* Paragraph 96.
[171] *Ibid.* Paragraph 104.
[172] Article I (1) (c) of the USA-Turkey BIT defines investment as: "any right conferred by law or contract, and any licenses and permits pursuant to law".

Turkey BIT, there are three circumstances in which a dispute shall be deemed as an "investment dispute". Indeed, this article defined an investment dispute as:

"a dispute involving (a) the interpretation or application of an investment agreement between a Party and a national or company of the other Party; (b) the interpretation or application of any investment authorization granted by a Party's foreign investment authority to such national or company; or (c) an alleged breach of any right conferred or created by this Treaty with respect to an investment."

The PSEG asserted that the dispute in this case involved the interpretation and application of the Contract and also the interpretation or application of the investment authorization granted by Turkey. The dispute fell within the terms of Article VI of the USA-Turkey BIT, thus the jurisdictional requirement of Article 25(1) of the ICSID Convention was met as the dispute arose directly from the investment.

In fact, the Tribunal found that the dispute in the Turkey case fell absolutely within the definition of an "investment dispute" as provided in paragraphs (a) and (b) of Article VI (1) of the Treaty. The Tribunal, in reaching its decision, placed much emphasize on the validity of Contract. Due to the fact that the Contract was valid and binding, the Tribunal found that the Contract was considered an investment agreement under which the investor was authorized to undertake the activities stipulated in that. In particular, the Tribunal found that Article 4 and 35 of the Contract provides the activities that investor should undertake. In addition, the Tribunal held that the proper authorization was issued to the PSEG by the Turkish investment authority, first in the form of a branch office and later as a limited liability company.

In Paragraph 121 of the Award, the Tribunal found that the dispute involves questions of interpretation or application of both the investment agreement and the investment authorization. Therefore, the Tribunal held that on the basis of the definition of "investment dispute" in the USA- Turkey BIT, the dispute in this case arose directly out of an investment, thus the jurisdictional requirements under Article 25(1) of the ICSID Convention are satisfied.

3.   Notification Regarding Consent to ICSID, Article 25 (4) of the Convention

Turkey contested that even if there was an investment, there is no consent to jurisdiction, since Turkey had a notification to the ICSID Centre in accordance with the Article 25 (4) of the ICSID Convention. Indeed, pursuant to this article, parties may "notify the Centre of the class or classes of disputes which it would or would not consider submitting to the jurisdiction of the Centre..."[173]   Thus, Turkey notified the Secretary General of ICSID on February 23, 1989 that "only the disputes arising directly out of investment activities which have obtained necessary permission, in conformity with the relevant legislation of the Republic of Turkey on foreign capital, and that have effectively started shall be subject to the jurisdiction of the Centre".[174] Turkey argued that the investment project never "effectively started", thus the consent to arbitration is absent.[175]   Conversely, the PSEG contended that the notifications under the Article 25 (4) of the ICSID Convention do not have a legally binding effect since this article precisely provides that "Such notifications shall not constitute the consent required by paragraph (1)".

The Tribunal examined the essential question raised by Turkey regarding the legal extent of notifications under Article 25 (4) of the ICSID Convention.   The Tribunal rightly found that Article 25 (4) of the ICSID Convention does not grant any legal effect to notifications as it refers to the disputes that the Contracting Parties "would or would not consider submitting to the jurisdiction of the Centre" since the issue of consent is left to instruments such as investment agreements and bilateral investment treaties.

The Tribunal held that the notification procedure was "for information purposes". [176] In fact, like most legal scholars arguments, the Report on the Convention by the Bank's Executive Directors also elucidated that notifications would "serve for purposes of information only" and not constitute reservations to the ICSID Convention.[177]

In Paragraph 140 of the Award, the Tribunal held that in the case of doubt, the notification will be useful for the construing of parties' consent but it does not have an "autonomous legal operation".[178]   Notifications are basically an instrument that allows States to articulate questions of policy to which they are not bound and that do not create rights for the other parties.[179]   It is essential to note that the notifications should be included in the consent that the Contracting Party will later give in its investment

---

[173] See Article 25 of the ICSID Convention.
[174] *Ibid.* Paragraph 125.
[175] *Ibid.* Paragraph 126.
[176] Peterson, Eric Luke, Tribunal Upholds Jurisdiction in Investment Treaty Claim against Turkey, Investment Law and Policy Weekly News Bulletin, October 13, 2004, http://www.iisd.org/pdf/2004/investment_investsd_oct13_2004.pdf (visited 6.7.2007)
[177] *Ibid.* Paragraph 137.
[178] *Ibid.* Paragraph 141.
[179] *Ibid.* Paragraph 144.

agreements or bilateral investment treaties. Otherwise, the notification is not going to be effective.[180] In this case, Turkey gave its consent by USA-Turkey BIT, before the notification. Thus, in order to be effective, the contents of a notification should have been added by a Protocol to the USA-Turkey BIT. However, Turkey did not include its notification to USA-Turkey BIT.

To sum up, the Tribunal found that the notifications under Article 25 (4) of the ICSID Convention do not have a binding legal effect. Thus, Turkey's jurisdictional objection on this ground was dismissed.[181]

4.   Forum Selection Clauses and the Nature of Disputes: Contract based or Treaty based?

Turkey objected the jurisdiction of the Tribunal stated that the obligation under USA-Turkey BIT to resort any previously agreed dispute settlement procedure has not been met. Turkey argued that the PSEG had the obligation to resort to the agreed procedure before arbitration since Article VI (2) of the USA-Turkey BIT utilizes the verb "shall" and it mandates to investor to resort previously agreed procedure.[182] In fact, if the dispute cannot be resolved by consultations and negotiations, this article states, "the dispute shall be submitted for settlement in accordance with any previously agreed, applicable dispute settlement procedures". The second clause of this article provides that one year later a party may recourse to ICSID arbitration if " the dispute has not, for any reason, been submitted by the national or company for resolution in accordance with any applicable dispute settlement procedure previously agreed to by the parties to the dispute".

Turkey argued that the parties in this case had an agreement to a dispute settlement procedure. Even though the draft Contract submitted to the Danistay, Turkish High Administrative Court, had an ICSID arbitration clause, this clause was precisely deleted by that body on the understanding that the Danistay had exclusive jurisdiction over disputes regarding Concession Contracts under Turkish Law. Due to the fact that the PSEG did not submit the dispute to the Danistay, the PSEG does not have any right to submit dispute to the ICSID arbitration.[183]

---

[180] *Ibid.* paragraph 145.
[181] *Ibid.* Paragraph 147.
[182] *Ibid.* Paragraph 148.
[183] *Ibid.* Paragrapn 151.

The Tribunal held that there is no incompatibility between the Provisions of Article VI (2) and Article VI (3) of the USA-Turkey BIT. These articles provide step by step dispute settlement mechanism.[184] Pursuant to the USA-Turkey BIT dispute settlement provision, the following sequence of dispute settlement mechanism is agreed by the parties: firstly consultations and negotiations are provided as an initial step. If this fails, if the parties agree, third party non-binding procedure can be applied. If this also fails, then the dispute shall be resorted to the previously agreed mechanism. If there was no submission to the previously agreed mechanism, then after one year, the investor can request for arbitration from ICSID. These steps of dispute settlement procedures are generally utilized mechanisms under international law.[185]

In reaching its decision, the Tribunal construed the wording of the dispute settlement provisions of USA-Turkey BIT. The Tribunal explained that Article VI (2) provides "shall" does not mean that investor has an obligation since the investor may not opt to solve the dispute at all. In Paragraph 161 of the Award, the tribunal stated that the investor has a right to choose to previously agreed mechanism. If the investor chooses to follow that mechanism, the dispute must then be submitted to that mechanism. Thus, in this context, "the "shall" become mandatory for the other party".[186] Because of this, Article VI (3) (a) clearly stipulates that the ICSID arbitration will not be available if the "national or company" has resorted the dispute to the previously agreed procedure.[187]

The Tribunal also concluded that there was no agreement on an exclusive dispute settlement mechanism stating that Danistay has an exclusive jurisdiction. Even if the Danistay has an exclusive jurisdiction under Turkish law, there are still some reliable arguments against its jurisdiction. Firstly, the amended Turkish laws provided that Concession Contracts could be submitted to international arbitration. Secondly, and the most essential issue in this case is that the dispute is treaty dispute not a contract dispute.

Article 90 of the Turkish Constitution, states "International agreements duly put into effect carry the force of law...". In other words, under the Turkish Constitutional system, treaties at least rank equally with the law. Thus, if there is a treaty and dispute is related with that treaty, that treaties' dispute settlement procedure is going to be

---

[184] *Ibid.* Paragraph 159.
[185] *Ibid.* Paragraph 160.
[186] *Ibid.* Paragraph 161.
[187] *Ibid.* Paragraph 162.

applied. Indeed, in the Paragraph 168 of the Award, the Tribunal held that "...whatever the jurisdiction the Danistay might have had or still has in respect of administrative acts and concession contracts yields to treaty provisions which, in the instant case is the investment protection Treaty and associated arbitration." [188]

It is worthwhile to note that contract based disputes are different from treaty based disputes. This issue has been analyzed and discussed by numerous arbitral cases, as in, CMS, Aguas del Aconquija, Launder, Genin, etc. For example, in CMS case, the Tribunal held that *"as contractual claims are different from treaty claims, even if there had been or there currently was a recourse to the local courts for breach of contract, this would not have prevented submission of the treaty claim to arbitration"[189]*

After the interpretation of USA-Turkey BIT's dispute settlement provision, and analyzing the dispute in order to find out whether it is a treaty dispute or contract dispute, the Tribunal concluded that it has a jurisdiction and decided that Turkey's jurisdictional objection on this ground was dismissed.

5. Lack of Legal Standing

Turkey also objected to the jurisdiction of the Tribunal regarding the North American Coal Corporation (NACC) and the Project Company on the ground that they did not have legal standing. Turkey contended that NACC did not have any investment in Turkey and any rights under the Concession Contract which was not signed by the said company. Furthermore, Turkey argued that the NACC had only one link with this case. That was the Memorandum of Understanding signed on August 1, 1998 between PSEG and NACC.[190]

As we mentioned in Chapter 2, the legal persons' standing sometimes can be controversial issue in the arbitration proceeding, as it was in case. With regard to the Project Company, Turkey asserted that it was not a company of the United States as required by the USA-Turkey BIT. Under Article VI (6) of the USA-Turkey BIT a company incorporated in Turkey "must have existed before the events giving rise to dispute for it to be considered a national of the United States". [191] However, in this case, Turkey rightly argued that the Project Company was incorporated in August 1999, two years after the disputed events.

---

[188] *Ibid.* Paragraph 168.
[189] *Ibid.* Paragraph 170.
[190] *Ibid.* Paragraph 175.
[191] *Ibid.* Paragraph 177.

In respect of the Project Company, the Tribunal found that the company had a legal standing. The Project Company had changed its corporate structure from a branch office of a foreign investor (PSEG) in Turkey to the new corporation because of the tax policies and other issues. The change of corporate structure has caused long negotiation between Turkey and PSEG. The Tribunal held that the Project Company can be considered the successor the earlier branch office, and branch offices' rights or interest were transferred to the new company. In addition, the aims of the Project Company as explained in the act of incorporation were explicitly linked to the investment.[192] With regard to Turkey's argument on the date of the events leading to the dispute, the Tribunal found that there were events after the incorporation date which involved a dispute between the parties.

In respect of the NACC, the Tribunal held that the company did not have a legal standing. Thus, Turkey's objection to jurisdiction regarding the NACC is accepted. In reaching its decision, the Tribunal explained the status of the NACC in the project. The NACC participated in the project in 1996 to assist in developing mining aspects of the power project, and in 1998, it purportedly joined PSEG as an equity investment by means of the Memorandum. Although the NACC participated in the preparation of mining plans, it had direct contract with PSEG, not with the Turkish Government. It is essential to note that the Memorandum granted the "option" to NACC to acquire ownership interest in the Project Company by means of a Shareholders Agreement to be negotiated later. In reaching its decision, the Tribunal agreed Turkey's argument that "options" can not be construed as an "investment" under the USA-Turkey BIT.[193] As we mentioned in Chapter 2, the definition of investment is an essential issue for substantive and procedural rights stipulated in bilateral investment treaties. Even though the arbitral tribunals generally interpret the definition of investment in broadly, the different circumstance of the case may lead this interpretation in a narrow way.

C.   **Merits of the Case**

As the Tribunal listed in the award[194], there were many contracts that some of them were not deemed a contact by Turkey (Respondent). There was a feasibility study approved by Ministry of Energy in 1995 and an implementation contract concluded in

---

[192] *Ibid.* Paragraph 184.
[193] *Ibid.* Paragraph 189.
[194] PSEG Global Inc. and Konya Ilgın Elektrik Üretüm ve Ticaret Limited Şirketi and Turkey, ICSID Case No. ARB/02/05, AWARD, January 19, 2007.

August 1996. Moreover, the Revised Mine Plan was submitted to Ministry of Energy in December 1997 and than a concession contract signed by the Project Company in December 1998 and Ministry of Energy in 1999. The Understanding of the commercial terms of the contracts defined in the opinion of the claimants and the respondents. Basically, respondent claimed that there was no meeting of mind with respect to contract, thus there was not any valid and binding contract at all. This was followed by disagreements with regard to the estimated costs of the project as a whole. In addition, there were other arguments pertaining to Treasury guarantees, energy sales agreements and fund agreements all of which never came to completion.

The Tribunal undertook the difficult task to evaluate the facts of the case in accordance with the opinions of both parties and learned experts and statements of numerous witnesses and many documents submitted by both PSEG and Turkey. It is worthwhile to note that the main disagreements regarding the Project occurred after the Revised Mine Plan was submitted by the Claimant in December 1997. Since after the revised mine plan was submitted to the Ministry of Energy, the overall cost of the project would increase in a great amount. The Tribunal found that an investment made in the form of a Concession Contract. However, in this case, except for groundbreaking ceremony, there was no mining undertaken and construction started, "not even in terms of the necessary preparations to that effect".[195] Nevertheless, this might not exclude to grant compensation for the existence of damages.

1.   **Main Arguments Regarding Violations of the USA-Turkey BIT**

In Paragraph 220 of the Award, the Tribunal rightly stated that as it became customary in investment arbitration, the aggrieved party incorporates the breach of every BIT clause with respect to the standards of the investor's protection, whereas the respondent strongly denies any breach.[196] In this case, apart from not claiming direct expropriation of the investment, PSEG followed the custom. PSEG asserted that Turkey violated the standard of fair and equitable treatment, failed to provide full protection and security, failed to refrain from arbitrary and discriminatory measures, and failed to observe the obligations it entered into with respect to investment.[197] In addition, PSEG argued that the investment was expropriated through measures

---

[195] *Ibid.* Paragraph 304.
[196] *Ibid.* Paragraph 220.
[197] *Ibid.* Paragraph 221.

equivalent to expropriation. Turkish Government denied any breach of the USA-Turkey BIT.

Apart from accepting that Turkey violated the fair and equitable treatment standard of USA-Turkey BIT, the Tribunal rejected all other PSEG arguments with regard to violations of USA-Turkey BIT. In particular, the tribunal concluded that in this case, there was no indirect or regulatory expropriation since this would require deprivation of the investor's control of their investment. However, in this case, there was no some form of deprivation and no any taking property. The Tribunal, in Paragraph 279 of the Award, also stated that "Although measures tantamount to expropriation may well make the question of ownership irrelevant, it does require a strong interference with clearly defined contract rights that in this case were in the end incomplete".[198] Thus, the tribunal found that Turkey did not breach expropriation provision of the USA-Turkey BIT.

2.   Fair and Equitable Treatment

PSEG contended that Turkey violated the fair and equitable treatment obligations under the USA-Turkey BIT. Article II (3) of the USA-Turkey BIT states that "Investments shall at all times be accorded fair and equitable treatment...in a manner consistent with international law". In addition, the Preamble of the USA-Turkey BIT states that such treatment is "desirable in order to maintain a stable framework for investment and maximum effective utilization of economic resources...."[199] On the contrary; Turkey argued that it acted in an equitable and reasonable manner, in good faith and full compliance with the domestic law. Thus, there was no breach of the fair and equitable treatment standard under the USA-Turkey BIT.[200]

With regard to the fair and equitable treatment, the tribunal did find out various breaches by Turkey of that USA-Turkey BIT obligation. In reaching its decision, the Tribunal began its examination by affirming that the claimant does not have to show that respondent act in a bad faith since the government might act in good faith but still does not fulfill its to duty to treat foreign investors fairly and equitably.[201] In this case,

---

[198] *Ibid.* Paragraph 279.
[199] See USA-Turkey BIT.
[200] See Claimants and Respondents detailed arguments at Paragraph 223-237.
[201] Diaz Cabrera Fernando & Peterson Eric Luke, Award handed down in Turkish Power Project Dispute at ICSID, Investment Treaty News, http://www.iisd.org/pdf/2007/itn_feb1_2007.pdf (visited 6.7.2007).

although the Tribunal found no evidence of bad faith on Turkey's activities, it held that the fair and equitable treatment standard was breached, and that breach was enough to be liable.

Firstly, the Tribunal found that there was an administrative negligence during the negotiations with the Claimants."[202] Among other things, the Tribunal determined that the following events were deemed serious administrative negligence and inconsistency: "key points of disagreement went unanswered and were not disclosed in a timely manner, silence was kept when there was evidence of such persisting and aggravating disagreement..." Thus, Turkey did not handle the negotiations with the PSEG in a professional and competent manner.

Secondly, in view of abuse of authority by the Turkish Government, the Tribunal found that there was a breach of the obligation to accord fair and equitable standard treatment. In particular, after the PSEG application regarding the new Law 4501, the Ministry of Energy and Natural Resources sought to initiate renegotiations of the Contract which was not in line with the purpose of the Law.[203] In addition, the Tribunal found that Turkish Government's demand of renegotiation of Contract was not within its authority. It is worthwhile to note that on January 22, 2000, Turkish Parliament enacted a new Law, Law No. 4501 which grants parties to convert existing concession contracts to private law contracts. In addition, this law allows the parties to revise old concession contracts in order to incorporate an international arbitration clause. The PSEG applied to the Ministry to convert the Concession Contract to a private law contract or to revise the Contract agreeing to submission of disputes to international arbitration. Nevertheless, the Ministry did not take into account of PSEG's application and without its authority, the Ministry demanded changes in the Contract. Therefore, this broader renegotiation demand was considered violation of the standard of fair and equitable treatment under the USA-Turkey BIT.[204]

Thirdly, the Tribunal found that the fair and equitable treatment obligation was breached because of the "roller-coaster" effect of the perpetual changes in the Turkish legislation.[205] Notably, among other things, the following issues were constantly changed due to the continuing legislative amendments: "the conditions governing the corporate status of the Project, and the constant alternation between private law status

---

[202] *Ibid.* Paragraph 246.
[203] *Ibid.* Paragraph 247.
[204] *Ibid.* Paragraph 247-249.
[205] *Ibid.* Paragraph 250.

and administrative concessions that went back and forth."[206] Although the aims of these amendments were to facilitate investment and protect investors, the administrative bodies failed to comply with the requirements of these new laws. Thus, the Tribunal pointed out that "it was not only the law that kept changing but notably the attitudes and policies of the administration."[207]

D.   Award

The Tribunal concluded that Turkey breached its obligation to accord the investor the fair and equitable treatment stipulated in Article II (3) of the USA-Turkey BIT. Since continually changing legislation environment, administrative negligence during negotiations with the PSEG and unauthorized demands by the Turkish Government for renegotiation of the Contract were considered a breach of the fair and equitable treatment provision.

The Claimants assessment of their losses pertaining to fair market value, loss of profits and the amount of their investments amounted to 494 million US Dollars. The Tribunal dismissed any compensation at all for fair market value and for loss of profits. The logic is arguable. The Tribunal rightly contended that bilateral investment treaties provide for the fair market value as the measure for compensation only with respect to expropriation because the Tribunal found that there was no expropriation in this case, the fair market value was not considered as a measure for compensation. In respect of loss of profits, the Tribunal rightly examined that ICSID Tribunals refused the awarding loss profits where there was no established record of profits.[208] In this case, the Tribunal held that the parties did not finalize the essential commercial terms of the Contract and if it decides the loss of profits, "the future profits would then be wholly speculative and uncertain."[209]

The Tribunal allowed however 11 million US Dollars in compensation for investment expenses but after various deductions, this came down to 9 million US Dollars and was awarded only to PSEG and not the Project Company itself since the Project Company is wholly owned by PSEG.[210] This means that the Tribunal, while

---

[206] *Ibid.* Paragraph 250.
[207] *Ibid.* Paragraph 254.
[208] See Paragraph 310-311.
[209] *Ibid.* Paragraph 313.
[210] *Ibid.* Paragraph 340.

acknowledging that Turkey owned compensation to PSEG for the failure of the investment project, the amount of compensation fall far short of what PSEG asserted.

II.   Pending Cases against Turkey Regarding Energy Sector

It must be noted that there are pending cases under the ICSID against Turkey with respect to Energy sector. Due to the fact that few details of these cases are in the public domain, we will just explain facts of these cases and some other issues that will arise in the arbitration proceedings.   It is true that ICSID did not reveal any comprehensive information regarding these cases since the confidentiality of the international arbitration proceeding is an essential factor that the institutional forum should provide.

A.   Libananco Holdings Co. Limited v. Republic of Turkey

1.   General Aspects of the Case

Libananco Holdings Co. Limited, a Cypriot company, requested an arbitration claim under the Energy Charter Treaty against Turkey.   The ICSID registered the case.[211]   Libananco, a Cypriot company, argued that it had an ownership interest in, *Cukurova Elektrik Anonim Sirketi (CEAS) and Kepez Elektrik Turk Anonim Sirketi (KEPEZ),* two electric utility companies in Turkey. Libananco asserted that the Turkish Government unlawfully seized and expropriated the facilities and assets of CEAS and KEPEZ in June 2003. Thus, Libanco claimed that its interest in these companies is also expropriated. Because of the financial reasons, Turkey had to take over the CEAS and KEPEZ. In this case, the ICSID Tribunal is going to evaluate and decide as to whether it has a jurisdiction or not.

Firstly, Turkey certainly is going to object the ICSID Tribunal Jurisdiction since there are strong arguments to Libananco's legal standing. This company has a strong tie with the Uzans who are the owner of the CEAZ and KEPEZ and has a really bad reputation in international legal and finance environment. For example, Libananco stated that one of its director names is Ali Cenk Turkkan, who has been acting as a proxy for Uzan family on numerous occasions. Turkey will claim that the Uzan family

---

[211] http://www.worldbank.org/icsid/cases/pending.htm (visited 6.7.2007).

was at the same time seller and the buyer of the transactions regarding the Libananco's acquisition of CEAS and KEPEZ shares.[212]

Secondly, the other question will arise in the arbitration proceeding as to whether Libananco made a legitimate investment in Turkey by acquiring the CEAS and KEPEZ shares under applicable Turkish, Cypriot, and other applicable laws.[213] Due to the financial conditions of the Uzan's family, how the Libananco acquire CEAS and Kepez stock is an interesting question. Even the Libananco asserted that it acquired CEAS and Kepez stock between October 2002 and May 2003, but it did not mention from whom and how it acquired them. It only submitted one document which is signed by its corporate secretary, containing a bare statement that its own shares of CEAS and KEPEZ.[214] The certification date of the document is February 2006, which is after the so called disputed occurred. It can be argued that the acquisitions of the CEAS and KEPEZ shares will be scrutinized under the applicable money laundering laws.

Thirdly, Turkey will object to ICSID jurisdiction due to the fact that there was no consent to ICSID Jurisdiction which is required and explained in Article 25 of the ICSID Convention.[215] According to Energy Charter Treaty, Turkey consented to the international arbitration of a dispute with an investor of another contracting party to the ICSID. However, the investment arbitration in accordance with ICSID is only available, if the investor has not submitted the dispute to the Turkish courts. This issue will probably be raised by Turkish government in the jurisdictional phrase of the Tribunal.

It should be noted that in this case ICSID arbitration was provided in the Energy Charter Treaty. Even though this treaty is multinational treaty, it is really essential to briefly explain this treaty in this part since it is really important for investment disputes on energy sector.

2.   General Knowledge of Energy Charter Treaty

The Energy Charter Treaty was signed in December 1994 and entered into legal force in April 1998 in order to promote and protect investment in energy sector.[216] The

---

[212] Eren Law Firm, Case Commentary, http://www.erenlaw.com/news/cc_libananco-turkey_icsid_0506.htm (visited 6.7.2007
[213] *Ibid.*
[214] *Ibid.*
[215] *Ibid.*
[216] Energy Charter Secretariat, The Energy Charter Treaty and Related Documents, A Legal Framework for International Energy Cooperation, 2004, p.39.

main objective of the Energy Charter Treaty is to strengthen the rule of law on energy issues and to mitigate risks associated with energy related investments.[217] In fact, one of the main provisions of the Treaty for the protection of investors is its dispute settlement mechanism.[218]

It is worthwhile to note that the Treaty deals not only with investment but also trade in energy materials. Thus there are provisions regarding energy products based on the World Trade Organization rules. With respect to investment, the Treaty mainly provides that each Contracting States should promote, protect and treat investment based on non-discrimination principles.[219] The substantive provisions, when coupled with the dispute settlement provisions, are capable of offering effective protection to foreign investors in energy sectors. Thus, the Treaty has contemporary and comprehensive dispute settlement provisions.

It can be observed that dispute settlement mechanism of the Treaty is similar to most BITs. It has dispute settlement procedures for cases of investment related disputes between an investor and a Contracting Party (Investor v State), and for disputes regarding the application or interpretation of the Energy Charter Treaty between Contracting Parties (State v State). Like recently signed BITs, the Energy Charter Treaty provides that foreign investors have direct right to bring a claim against host state concerning breach of an obligation of the Contracting Party under Part III of the Treaty.[220] Article 26 of the Treaty provides direct application of arbitration for foreign investors against Contracting States, "irrespective of any specific arbitral agreement between the parties."[221] Article 26 (2) of the Treaty provides investors with the option to submit disputes:

a.   to the courts or administrative tribunals of the state party to the dispute;

b.   in accordance with any applicable, previously agreed dispute settlement procedure; or

c.   international arbitration in accordance with the Article 26 of this Treaty

Furthermore, Article 26 (4) provides the investor with three options for arbitration: Arbitration according to the Rules of the ICSID Convention, a sole arbitrator or ad hoc arbitration tribunal established under the Arbitration rules of

---

[217] *Ibid.* p.14.
[218] See Article 26 and 27 of the Energy Charter Treaty
[219] See Article 10 of the Energy Charter Treaty.
[220] See Article 26 of the Energy Charter Treaty.
[221] Gillian Turner, <u>Investment Protection Through Arbitration: The Dispute Resolution Provisions of The Energy Charter Treaty</u>, International Arbitration Law Review, 1998, p.167.

UNCITRAL, and "arbitral proceeding under the Arbitration Institute of the Stockholm Chamber of Commerce".[222]

It is essential to note that by Article 26 (3), various states such as Turkey have refused to consent to the submission of a dispute under this Treaty's arbitration mechanism, if an investor has previously submitted the dispute either to the Courts or administrative tribunals of the state party to the dispute, or previously agreed dispute settlement mechanism. As explained above, in *Libananco* case, Turkey will probably argue that the Libananco had already submitted the dispute in Turkish Courts, thus, it can not submit the dispute to the ICSID because of the Article 26 (3) of the Treaty.

B.   Cementownia "Nowa Huta" S.A. v. Republic of Turkey[223]

It is interesting to note that this case has similar facts and arguments of Libananco case. Cementownia argued that its share in the KEPEZ and CEAS utilities are expropriated by Turkish government on political grounds. ICSID arbitration was provided for in bilateral investment treaty signed between Poland and Turkey.[224] On the contrary, Turkey argued that it expropriated these utilities because of the financial reasons.[225] In addition, Turkey asserted that this company has strong ties with Uzan family. Thus, like the above mentioned grounds on objections to ICSID in Libananco case, Turkey will and should challenge the ICSID jurisdiction claiming that there is no investment and the company does not have legal standing.

C.   Europe Cement Investment and Trade S.A. v. Republic of Turkey

This case is registered in ICSID, shortly after the Cementownia case.[226] Like Cementownia and Libananco cases, Europe Cement case has similar facts and issues. Europe Cement asserted that Turkey expropriated KEPEZ and CEAS utilities for political reasons.[227] Its claims based on the Turkish Government violation of Poland-Turkey BIT since it has minority stake in the KEPEZ and CEAS.[228] As explained in the above, Turkey most probably will object to ICSID jurisdiction on the same grounds of

---

[222] *Ibid.* P. 168.
[223] http://www.worldbank.org/icsid/cases/pending.htm (visited 6.7.2007).
[224] The American Lawyer, Arbitration Scorecard 2007: Top 50 Treaty Disputes, http://www.law.com/jsp/article.jsp?id=1181639136817 (visited 6.7.2007).
[225] *Ibid.*
[226] http://www.worldbank.org/icsid/cases/pending.htm (visited 6.7.2007).
[227] The American Lawyer, Arbitration Scorecard 2007: Top 50 Treaty Disputes, http://www.law.com/jsp/article.jsp?id=1181639136817 (visited 6.7.2007).
[228] *Ibid.*

Libananco and Cementownia cases that the Europe Cement is not an "investor", and there is no investment disputes at all.

CONCLUSION

BITs have played an important role in the development of international arbitration on investment disputes. As the main sources of international investment law, BITs include substantive and procedural rules so as to provide investment security and investment neutrality to foreign investment. In particular, through its investor-state dispute settlement provision the BITs recognized private companies as international subjects, since these provisions allow foreign investors to sue states directly.

This dissertation explained investor-state dispute settlement provisions of the BITs. Most BITs provides general provisions regarding investor-state dispute settlement procedures. In particular, by giving Turkey's BIT experiences this dissertation concludes that Turkey sign many BITs with other countries which have different provisions on investor-state dispute settlement. Moreover, we contend that the wording of the clauses in the BITs is also important for effective dispute settlement procedure.

The recent institutional and ad hoc arbitral decisions caused the novel developments on the BITs. For this reason, there are also some additional requirements which are regulated in the investor-state dispute settlement provisions of the BITs. An increasing number of BITs have provisions which state arbitration procedures more detailed. After looking through nearly all of the BITs, it can be mentioned clearly that while some of the BITs dedicated just only one article, some other contains a whole investor-state dispute settlement section with very detailed 10 articles regarding arbitration procedure. It shows that contracting parties' seek in making specific regulations so that they can rely on predictability in their implementation.

We can argue that the ICSID arbitration is the starting and the main step for the development of arbitration in international investment disputes. Indeed, recently this arbitration mechanism is extensively utilized. ICSID arbitration have different characteristic from other types of international commercial arbitration. In particular, the ICSID convention provides an effective system of enforcement of awards since they are recognized as final in all states parties to the convention. In addition, ICSID arbitration proceedings are independent of the intervention of domestic courts.

Due to the fact that there are new approaches on BITs and the increasing number of investor state dispute arbitrations, ICSID amended its rules of procedure for arbitration proceedings. The main objective of these amendments is to improve and provide effective and efficient ICSID arbitration process. In fact, ICSID amendments provide transparency through requiring publication of awards and allowing amicus curiae submission by third parties. Furthermore, the ICSID amended arbitration rules regarding provisional measures in order to provide fast-track procedures for interim relief. It should be noted that their impact and effectiveness on the development of international arbitration is going to be seen.

As a case study, this dissertation analyzed the ICSID cases against Turkey regarding energy sector. We summarized and evaluated the PSEG Global v. Turkey case so as to illustrate the practical aspects of the main requirements of investor state dispute settlement procedure such as, the definition of investment disputes, consent etc. Although Turkey enacted new laws to develop its energy sector providing more secure environment for foreign investors, consequences of losing ICSID cases will be a negative impact on Turkey's financial situation. To sum up, after analyzing ICSID cases against Turkey, this study shows that the investor-state dispute settlement mechanism and its main requirements are developed through not only by the phenomenon of the increasing number of BITs, but also mostly by institutional arbitration practices such as ICSID.

BIBLIOGRAPHY

BOOKS

Black's Law Dictionary, 8 th Edition, Thomson West, 2004.

Caliskan Yusuf, The Development of International Investment Law: Lessons From The OECD MAI Negotiations And Their Application to a Possible Multilateral Agreement on Investment, Washington University School of Law, Jurist Science Doctorate (JSD) Dissertation, 2002.

Collins Lawrence, Morse C G J, McClean David, Briggs Adrian, Harris Jonathan, McLachlan Campbell, Dicey, Morris & Collins on the Conflict of Laws, 14th Edition, Sweet & Maxwell, 2006.

Don R.Y, Protection of Foreign Investment under International Law, 1979.

Dolzer Rudolf & Stevens Margrete, Bilateral Investment Treaties, Martinus Nijhoff Publishers, 1995.

Energy Charter Secretariat, The Energy Charter Treaty and Related Documents, A Legal Framework for International Energy Cooperation, 2004.

Loibl Gerhard, International Economic Law, Evans D. Malcolm (Ed.), International Law, Second Edition, 2006.

Redfern Alan, Hunter Martin, Law and Practice of International Commercial Arbitration, Fourth Edition, London, Sweet and Maxwell, 2004.

Sornaraj M., The International Law on Foreign Investment, Second Edition, Cambridge University Press, 2004.

United Nations Conference on Trade and Development (UNCTAD), Bilateral Investment Treaties 1995-2006: Trends In Investment Rule Making, United Nations, New York and Geneva, 2007.

UNCTAD, Dispute Settlement: Investor-State, United Nations, New York and Geneva ,2003.

UNCTAD, Course on Dispute Settlement International Centre For Settlement of Investment Disputes, United Nations, New York and Geneva, 2003.

UNCTAD, Investor-State Disputes Arising From Investment Treaties: A Review, 2005.

Wolfgang Peter, Arbitration and Renegotiation of International Investment Agreements, Martinus Nijhoff Publishers, 1986.

ARTICLES

Caruba L. Sandra, Resolving International Investment Disputes in a Globalised World, New Zealand Business Law Quarterly, June 2007, p.128-130.

Diaz Cabrera Fernando & Peterson Eric Luke, Award handed down in Turkish Power Project Dispute at ICSID, Investment Treaty News, http://www.iisd.org/pdf/2007/itn_feb1_2007.pdf (visited 6.7.2007).

Eren Law Firm, Case Commentary, http://www.erenlaw.com/news/cc_libananco-turkey_icsid_0506.htm (visited 6.7.2007).

Fietta Stephen, Most Favoured Nation Treatment and Dispute Resolution Under Bilateral Investment Treaties: A Turning Point, International Arbitration Law Review, 2005, 131-138.

Finizio Steven P, Mortensen Julian Davis, Shenkman Ethan G, Recent Developments in Investor-State Arbitration: Effective Use of Provisional Measures, The European Arbitration Review, p.2.

Freyer Dana H., Garfinkel Barry H., Bilateral Investment Treaties and Arbitration, Dispute Resolution Journal, 1998, p. 75.

Gillian Turner, Investment Protection Through Arbitration: The Dispute Resolution Provisions of The Energy Charter Treaty, International Arbitration Law Review, 1998, p.167.

Gottwald Eric, Leveling The Playing Field: Is It Time for a Legal Assistance Center for Developing Nations in Investment Treaty Arbitration?, American University International Law Review, 2007, p.246-247.

Harten Van Gus, Loughlin Martin, Investment Treaty Arbitration As a Species of Global Administrative Law, European Journal of International Law, February 2006, p.124.

Kishoiyian Bernard, The Utility of Bilateral Investment Treaties in the Formulation of Customary International law, Nortwestern Journal of International Law and Business, Winter 1994, p.350.

Lauterpacht Elihu, International Law and Private Foreign Investment, Indiana Journal of Global Legal Studies, Spring 1997, p.266.

Legum Barton, Investment Treaty Arbitration's Contribution To International Commercial Arbitration, Dispute Resolution Journal, August-October, 2005 p.73-74.

Lopina A. David, The International Centre For Settlement of Investment Disputes: Investment Arbitration for the 1990s., Ohio State Journal on Dispute Resolution, 1988, p 110.

Mehren von M. George, Salomon T. Claudia, Navigating Through Investor-State Arbitrations an Overview of Bilateral Investment Treaty Claims, Dispute Resolution Journal, 2004, p. 71.

Mutharika A. Peter, Creating an Attractive Investment Climate in the Common Market for Eastern and Southern Africa (COMESA) Region, Foreign Investment Law Journal, ICSID Review, 1997, p.272.

Nmehielle Vincent O. Orlu, Enforcing Arbitration Awards Under the International Convention For the Settlement of Investment Disputes (ICSID Convention), Annual Survey of International and Comparative Law, Spring 2001, p.30.

OECD Investment Committee, Transparency and Third Party Participation in Investor-State Dispute Settlement Procedures, Working Papers on International Investment, Number 2005/1.

Peterson, Eric Luke, Tribunal Upholds Jurisdiction in Investment Treaty Claim against Turkey, Investment Law and Policy Weekly News Bulletin, October 13, 2004, http://www.iisd.org/pdf/2004/investment_investsd_oct13_2004.pdf (visited 6.7.2007).

Santens Ank, ICSID Amends Its Arbitration Rules, International Arbitration Law Review, 2006, p.120.

Seriki Hakeem, Umbrella Clauses and Investment Treaty Arbitration: All Encompassing or Respite for Sovereign States and State Entities, Journal of Business Law, 2007.

Siquerios Jose Luis, Bilateral Treaties on the Reciprocal Protection of Foreign Investment, California Western International Law Journal, Spring 1994, p.257.

Sureda Andres Rigo, Two Views on ICSID Arbitration, World Arbitration and Mediation Report, June 2002, p.166.

The American Lawyer, Arbitration Scorecard 2007: Top 50 Treaty Disputes.

Vandevelde J. Kenneth, Investment Liberalization and Economic Development: The Role of Bilateral Investment Treaties, Colombia Journal of Transnational Law, 1998, p.507-514.

Vandevelde J Kenneth, The BIT Program: A Fifteen-Year Appraisal, The Development and Expansion of Bilateral Investment Treaties, American Society of International Law Proceedings, 1992, p. 533.

Yannaca-Small Katia , Improving the System of Investor-State Dispute Settlement: An Overview, OECD Working Papers on International Investment, Number 2006/1.

TREATIES

Agreement between The People's Republic of China and The Republic of Turkey Concerning The Reciprocal Promotion and Protection of Investments, http://www.unctad.org/sections/dite/iia/docs/bits/china_turkey.pdf

Agreement between The Republic of Turkey and The Federal Republic of Nigeria Concerning The Reciprocal Promotion and Protection of Investments, http://www.unctad.org/sections/dite/iia/docs/bits/turkey_nigeria.pdf

Agreement between The Republic of Tunisia and The Republic of Turkey Concerning The Reciprocal Promotion and Protection of Investments, http://www.unctad.org/sections/dite/iia/docs/bits/TurkeyTunisia.pdf

Turkey-United States: Treaty Concerning the Reciprocal Encouragement and Protection of Investments, http://www.unctad.org/sections/dite/iia/docs/bits/us_turkey.pdf

Agreement on Reciprocal Encouragement and Protection of Investments between the Kingdom of the Netherlands and the Republic of Turkey BIT, http://www.unctad.org/sections/dite/iia/docs/bits/netherlands_turkey.pdf

Treaty Between the United States of America and the Argentine Republic Concerning the Reciprocal Encouragement and Protection of Investment, http://www.unctad.org/sections/dite/iia/docs/bits/argentina_us.pdf

Agreement between the Government of the Russian Federation and the Government of the Republic of Turkey regarding the Promotion and Reciprocal Protection of Investments, http://www.unctad.org/sections/dite/iia/docs/bits/russia_turkey.pdf

Agreement between The Government of The Republic of Turkey and The Government of The Democratic and Popular Republic of Algeria Concerning The Reciprocal Promotion and Protection of Investments, http://www.unctad.org/sections/dite/iia/docs/bits/turkey_algeria.pdf

Agreement between The Government of The United Kingdom of Great Britain and Northern Ireland and The Government of The Republic of Turkey for The Promotion and Protection of Investments, http://www.unctad.org/sections/dite/iia/docs/bits/uk_turkey.pdf

USA BIT Model 2004, http://www.state.gov/documents/organization/38710.pdf

Turkey Model BIT, Agreement Between the Republic of Turkey and --------- Concerning the Reciprocal Promotion and Protection of Investments, http://www.unctad.org/sections/dite/iia/docs/Compendium//en/211%20volume%208.pdf

Agreement Between the Kingdom of Sweden and the Republic of Turkey on the Reciprocal Promotion and Protection of Investments, http://www.unctad.org/sections/dite/iia/docs/bits/sweden_turkey.pdf

Agreement between Romaina and The Republic of Turkey on the Reciprocal Promotion and Protection of Investments.
http://www.unctad.org/sections/dite/iia/docs/bits/romania_turkey.pdf

Agreement between the Lebanese Republic and the Republic of Turkey on the Promotion and Reciprocal Protection of Investments,
http://www.unctad.org/sections/dite/iia/docs/bits/lebanon_turkey.pdf

Agreement the Government of the Republic of Turkey and the Government of the Democratic and Popular Republic of Algeria Concerning the Reciprocal Promotion and Protection of Investments,
http://www.unctad.org/sections/dite/iia/docs/bits/turkey_algeria.pdf

Agreement between the Government of the Arab Republic of Egypt and the Government of the Republic of Chile on the Reciprocal Promotion and Protection of Investments, http://www.unctad.org/sections/dite/iia/docs/bits/chile_egypt.pdf

INTERNATIONAL INSTRUMENTS

ICSID, ICSID Convention, Regulations and Rules,
http://www.worldbank.org/icsid/basicdoc/intro.htm

UNIDROIT Principles of International Commercial Contracts, 1994.

The Rules of International Centre for Dispute Resolution (ICDR), www.adr.org .

The Rules of Arbitration of the International Chamber of Commerce (ICC),
http://www.iccwbo.org/court/english/arbitration/rules.asp.

UNCITRAL Arbitration Rules,
http://www.uncitral.org/pdf/english/texts/arbitration/arb-rules/arb-rules.pdf

CASES

PSEG Global Inc., The North American Coal Corporation, and Konya Ilgın Elektrik Üretim ve Ticaret Limited Şirketi (CLAIMANT) and Republic of Turkey (Respondent), Decision on Jurisdiction, ICSID Case No. ARB/02/5.

PSEG Global Inc. and Konya Ilgın Elektrik Üretüm ve Ticaret Limited Şirketi and Turkey, ICSID Case No. ARB/02/05, AWARD, January 19, 2007.

ICSID Case No. ARB/97/7, Decision of January 25, 2000.

ICSID Case No. ARB/02/13, Decision of November 15, 2004.

ICSID Case No. ARB/03/24, Decision of February 8, 2005.

CME Czech Republic B. V. v. Czech Republic Partial Award (September 13, 2001).

Lauder v.Czech Republic (Final Award) (September 3, 2002).

Decision on Jurisdiction (August 8, 2000) and Award (July 26, 2001) ICSID Case No. ARB/98/5.

www.ingramcontent.com/pod-product-compliance
Lightning Source LLC
Chambersburg PA
CBHW080526110426
42742CB00017B/3248